THE WAY OF LIFE SERIES

THE

MESSAGE

of

OLD TESTAMENT HISTORY

Volume Four

REHOBOAM TO NEHEMIAH

by John T. Willis

Published By
BIBLICAL RESEARCH PRESS
774 East North 15th Street
Abilene, Texas
79601

THE WAY OF LIFE SERIES

THE MESSAGE of
OLD TESTAMENT HISTORY

Volume 4, Rehoboam to Nehemiah

◇

◇

LIBRARY OF CONGRESS CATALOG CARD NO. 77-90653
I.S.B.N. 0-89112-144-7

◇

PREFACE

The historical period covered in this booklet is a little over 500 years: from the days of Jeroboam I and Rehoboam (beginning ca. 922 B. C.) to the time of Ezra, Nehemiah, and Malachi (ca. 458-400 B. C.). However, the primary purpose of this work is not to deal with historical matters (although some of the major historical events are discussed), but to emphasize leading spiritual and religious thoughts taught in and suggested by the biblical text.

We urge the reader to consult the Preface to Volume I in this series for suggestions as to how to use this booklet. Basically this thought needs to be emphasized: the present volume is intended as *a study guide* and not as an exhaustive treatment of the material under consideration; thus the student is urged to read supplemental materials, including the Bible (in a variety of modern English versions), good historical atlases, Old Testament histories, scholarly articles in Bible encyclopedias and journals on specific problems, commentaries, and more extensive Old Testament and Biblical theologies.

It is with a great deal of pleasure and admiration that I dedicate this little volume to some of my former students and their children, who have distinguished themselves by establishing strong Christian homes which are a model to their fellow-Christians and associates: Sherrill and Marion McConnell and their children Melanie, Michelle, and Melissa of Franklin, Tennessee; Robert (Buzzy) and Sharon Neil and their daughter Martha Ann of Portland, Tennessee; and Denny and Cynthia Saulsberry of Plymouth, Michigan. May God give us more families like these.

TABLE OF CONTENTS

Lesson   Page

Lesson I

THE FUTILITY OF POWER STRUGGLES AMONG GOD'S PEOPLE– JEROBOAM I AND REHOBOAM (II KINGS 12-14; II CHRONICLES 10-12)

"God is not a God of confusion but of peace" (I Corinthians 14:33)

I Kings 12-14 = *II Chronicles* 10-12 relate some of the immediate causes for the division between the ten northern tribes of Israel and the tribe of Judah. This lesson attempts to emphasize these causes and to make application to recurring church problems of today. It should be kept in mind that the seeds of division had been sown long before the conflict that erupted between Jeroboam I and Rehoboam. The sons of Jacob, from whom the different tribes of Israel descended, were frequently hostile to each other (see *Genesis* 37). During the lifetime of Joshua, there was suspicion and strife between the tribes east of Jordan and those west of Jordan (*Joshua* 22). In the time of the Judges, internal struggles between different tribes surfaced (*Judges* 8:1-3; 9:22-57; 12:1-6; 17-18; 19-21). During Saul's reign, the tribe of Judah, certain Israelites (even some belonging to Saul's own family!), and hired mercenaries of Saul followed David as a leader of a small band of renegades (see *I Samuel* 22:1-2; 30:26-31; *I Chronicles* 11:26-12:40). After Saul's death, Abner placed the ten northern tribes under the rule of Saul's son Ish-bosheth at Mahanaim, while David ruled over the tribe of Judah at Hebron (*II Samuel* 2:8-11). When David returned to Jerusalem after Absalom had been killed by Joab, the men of Israel and the men of Judah bickered over which of the two groups had priority to give him an official escort back to the capital (*II Samuel* 19:41-43). God raised up Jeroboam I of the tribe of Ephraim against Solomon to punish him for marrying foreign wives and worshipping their gods (*I Kings* 11:26-40). Consequently, the division between the ten northern tribes and Judah was the end product of a long period of internal strife among God's people. Man has not changed. Division in the church through the ages has often been the result of long struggles between self-seeking factions, and the same is true today.

Rehoboam Uses Poor Judgment in Dealing with People (I Kings 12:1-15; II Chronicles 10:1-15)
Strife often arises because powerful leaders do not use good judgment in dealing with the people that follow them. Rehoboam (922-915 B. C.) the son of Solomon was partly responsible for the division among God's people for this very reason. When Jeroboam I learns that Solomon is dead and that Rehoboam has gone to Shechem to be made king, he returns from Egypt (where he had fled to escape death at the hands of Solomon, see *I Kings* 11:40) and becomes the spokesman for the ten northern tribes. In their behalf, he goes to Rehoboam and asks that he lighten the hard service which Solomon had laid upon the people (see 5:13-17). The old counselors advise Rehoboam to "be a servant" to the people (12:7), to "be kind" to them (*II Chronicles* 10:7), and to lighten their burdens, while the young counselors urge him to assert his authority from the very first of his reign by refusing to yield one whit to the wishes of the people, and by increasing their burdens. Following the advice of the young men, Rehoboam returns to the people and speaks "harshly" to them (*I Kings* 12:13), saying, "My father chastised you with whips, but I will chastise you with scorpions" (12:11, 14).

Usually when there is division among men (whether it be in the home, in politics, or in religion), both parties are to blame to some extent. Rehoboam's fault is that of asserting his authority and of being insensitive to the circumstances and feelings of his fellowmen who look to him for leadership. Christians can learn an important lesson from this. Jesus "came not to be served but to serve" (*Matthew* 20:28), and thus he commands the respect and love of all of his true followers. And in instructing elders as to how they should deal

2

with the people committed to their charge, Peter writes: "not as domineering over those in your charge but being examples to the flock" (*I Peter* 5:3).

Israel Retaliates (I Kings 12:16-23; II Chronicles 10:16-11:4)

When they hear Rehoboam's stern dictum, the Israelites depart with bitter feelings against him and the entire Davidic dynasty. Rehoboam sends Adoram (Adoniram, 4:6; 5:14; Hadoram) to carry out the decree, and the Israelites stone him to death. Anger and bitterness lead to murder, and in fact are the sins of the heart which produce murder (see *Matthew* 5:21-26). How much wiser and more godlike it would have been for the oppressed Israelites to pray for Rehoboam, to submit to his unreasonable demands, and to treat him well whenever opportunity presented itself! The genuine child of God should respond in this way to those who mistreat him (*Proverbs* 25:21-22; *Matthew* 5:38-48; *Romans* 12:14-21; *I Corinthians* 6:1-8). Rehoboam gathers together the Judean army to go up against North Israel to avenge the death of Adoram, but the prophet Shemaiah comes to him and persuades him not to do this.

Jeroboam I and Rehoboam Both Forsake the Lord (I Kings 12:24-33; 14:21-24; II Chronicles 11:5-12:1)

Both Jeroboam I (922-901 B. C.) and Rehoboam lead their respective nations into apostasy from God, although each in his own way. Jeroboam reasons that if the North Israelites go to Jerusalem to worship as the Lord has decreed, they will soon abandon him as their king and return to the Davidic ruler. So he establishes a rival worship in North Israel designed to satisfy the people's religious yearnings. It consists of four basic elements, each of which represents a departure from the worship that God had specified.

First, he makes two calves of gold, which are understood to be or to represent the gods (or God) who brought them out of the land of Egypt (*I Kings* 12:28). At Ugarit in northern Syria, Baal was represented under the figure of a bull, and it may be that the Israelites were influenced by the Canaanites around them and transferred this concept of Baal to Yahweh. Aaron, perhaps under the influence of foreign people with whom the Israelites had come in contact, built a golden calf to represent Yahweh while Moses was on Mount

Sinai communing with God and receiving his commandments (*Exodus* 32:1-24). Whatever may have been the attraction of representing Yahweh under the figure of a bull, Jeroboam's action is in direct violation of the first two commandments (*Exodus* 20:1-6).

Second, Jeroboam designates Dan in the far north, and Bethel in the far south, of North Israel as the places where the Israelites are to worship (*I Kings* 12:29-30). This violates the divine choice of Zion or Jerusalem as the proper place for God's people to worship (see *Psalms* 76:2; 78:68; 132:13), and God had specified through Moses that the Israelites were to worship him only at the place that he would choose (*Deuteronomy* 12:5-11).

Third, Jeroboam drives the Levitical priests out of North Israel (*II Chronicles* 11:13-14), and appoints non-Levitical priests to oversee the worship (*I Kings* 12:31). He does this in spite of the fact that God had specified in the law that only the descendants of Levi were to transport the holy things of the sanctuary and to use them in religious service (*Numbers* 18).

Fourth, Jeroboam establishes a festival in North Israel on the fifteenth day of the eighth month as a rival to the Feast of Tabernacles which, according to God's decree, was to be observed on the fifteenth day of the seventh month (see *Leviticus* 23:33-36). Instead of encouraging the people to keep this feast on the month that God had commanded, Jeroboam charges them to observe it in the month "which he had devised of his own heart" (*I Kings* 12:32-33).

Undoubtedly most of the people viewed these changes as so slight and insignificant as to be unworthy of any serious concern. But to God they represented deliberate disobedience to his revealed will. So he sends a prophet of Judah to Bethel to cry out against the altar that Jeroboam had built there. He announces that some day a descendant of David named Josiah would become king of Judah and would burn the bones of the priests of the high places on this altar (13:2). When Jeroboam stretches out his hand to command his men to lay hold on the prophet, his hand withers. He begs the prophet to pray the Lord to restore his hand as it was before; the prophet does so, and the Lord restores it. The prophet gives Jeroboam a sign that his prediction concerning the altar would come to pass; the altar is torn down and the ashes on it poured out (13:1-6).

It is worthy of note that this prediction was made during the reign of Jeroboam I, so 922-901 B. C., but was not fulfilled until the eighteenth year of Josiah (623 B. C.) or later (*II Kings* 23:15-16; cf. 22:3). In other words, the Lord revealed to this prophet the name of a king and a deed that he would perform some 300 years before the fact. If this is possible, there is no reason to doubt that God could reveal to Old Testament prophets and inspired persons specific truths concerning Christ and the church hundreds of years before they occurred.

Rehoboam is no less guilty of apostasy from the Lord than is Jeroboam. It is true that he continues to worship in the city which God had chosen, Jerusalem, that he supports the Levitical priests, and that he observes the Feast of Tabernacles on the fifteenth day of the seventh month. But he is guilty of other evils. He adopts many of the customs of Canaanite Baalism which is being practiced by Israel's neighbors in the land, including worship on the high places, making pillars and Asherim as idols, and setting up male prostitutes which were used in fertility rites connected with Canaanite religion (*I Kings* 14:23-24); he forsake God's law (*II Chronicles* 12:1); and, like his father Solomon, he takes many wives and concubines, viz., 18 wives and 60 concubines (11:21).

There is an important message in this for modern man. On the one hand, man is in trouble spiritually when he refuses to comply with God's revealed commands, and substitutes in their place the devices of his own heart. This may apply to the substitution of sprinkling or pouring for immersion as Biblical baptism (the Greek word *baptizo* means "to immerse," and not "to sprinkle" or "to pour"; see *Acts* 8:38-39; *Romans* 6:3-4, for passages which clearly show that baptism is immersion, even to one that does not know Greek), or to the partaking of the Lord's Supper at some time other than the first day of the week as did the early Christians (see *Acts* 20:7 as well as the unanimous witness of early church history). On the other hand, man may adhere faithfully to commands involving external acts such as these, and still be unfaithful to God by compromising with the ways of immoral and ungodly people about him (see *Romans* 12:1-2). Either path constitutes infidelity to the Lord.

The Tragedy of Believing A Lie (I Kings 13:7-34)

When the prophet of Judah prays that the Lord will restore the withered hand of Jeroboam, Jeroboam invites him to go home with him to refresh himself and receive a present from the king. However, the prophet refuses because the Lord had told him not to eat bread or drink water at Bethel, nor to return by the way that he came. An old prophet of Bethel learns from his sons what had transpired, and he pursues the prophet of Judah. He invites him to return to his house to eat bread and drink water, and when he refuses he tells him that an angel of the Lord had told him to bring him to his house and to give him bread and water, but he is lying. The prophet of Judah is convinced that the old prophet is telling the truth, and so goes home with him. There the word of the Lord comes to the old prophet, and he declares that the prophet of Judah will die. On his way home, he is attacked by a lion and killed because he "disobeyed the word of the Lord" (verses 21, 26). The old prophet retrieves his body, buries him in his own grave, and charges his sons to bury him beside the dead prophet's bones because his prediction concerning the altar of Bethel would surely come to pass.

Frequently man is confronted with the problem of whether to believe a revealed divine truth or a convincing tenet of man. The account in *I Kings* 13:7-34 calls to mind Paul's words to the Galatians: "But even if we, or an angel from heaven, should preach to you a gospel contrary to that which we preached to you, let him be accursed" (*Galatians* 1:8). The inspired words of scripture alone are ultimately "profitable for teaching, for reproof, for correction, and for training in righteousness, that the man of God may be complete, equipped for every good work" (*II Timothy* 3:16-17). Any human dogma that deviates from this norm, no matter how convincing it may seem, must be sternly avoided.

Sin's Consequences (I Kings 14:1-20, 25-31; II Chronicles 12:2-16)

Like David and Solomon before them, and like all sinners, for awhile undoubtedly both Jeroboam and Rehoboam thought they had gotten away with their sins. But in due time, God punishes each of these kings severely. Jeroboam's little son becomes ill, and Jeroboam tells his wife to disguise herself and to go to the prophet Ahijah to find out what will happen to the child. The Lord tells Ahijah that she is coming, and when she arrives Ahijah tells her to return to Jeroboam and announce to him that because he did not keep God's commandments and follow him with all his heart, God would bring his dynasty to an abrupt end, and the child would die. He also declares that because of Jeroboam's unfaithfulness, God would root up the Israelites out of the land of Canaan and take time beyond the Euphrates as exiles in a foreign land. In fulfillment of these predictions: (1) the child died (14:17-18); (2) the dynasty of Jeroboam I ended when Baasha killed his son Nadab and seized the throne of North Israel (15:27-30); (3) the Israelites were carried into the Assyrian captivity by Sargon II in 721 B.C. (*II Kings* 17). As one reads the account of these events, he is reminded of the death of the illegitimate son of David and Bathsheba (*II Samuel* 12:14-23), and of the end of the dynasty of Saul because Saul did not wait for Samuel to arrive at Gilgal before offering the burnt offering (*I Samuel* 13:8-15), and because he did not obey God's command to utterly destroy the Amalekites (*I Samuel* 15).

Because of Rehoboam's apostasy for him, God raises up Shishak (Sheshonk I, ca. 940-915 B.C.) against him with the purpose of destroying Jerusalem and everything in it. Archeologists have discovered a fragment of a triumphal stela which Sheshonk erected at Megiddo to celebrate his victories over the southern and central regions of Palestine, and portions of an inscription on the wall of the temple of Amon at Karnak in Egypt listing the towns in Palestine and Syria that he overran. God sends the prophet Shemaiah to Rehoboam, saying, "You abandoned me, so I have abandoned you to the hand of Shishak" (*II Chronicles* 12:5). Rehoboam and the princes of Israel are convicted of their sins and humble themselves before the Lord. Then the Lord declares that he will not allow Shishak to utterly destroy the city, but will make Judah subject to Egypt. Shishak carried away the treasures of the temple and of the king's palace, and the shields of gold that Solomon had made, but the city of Jerusalem is spared.

It is significant that the key figures in the reigns of Jeroboam and Rehoboam are not really kings, but the prophets that God sent to them at critical times. The prophet Ahihah from Shiloh figures prominently in two major events in Jeroboam's career: (1) he tears his garment into twelve pieces and gives ten to Jeroboam, signifying that he will become king over the ten northern tribes after Solomon's death (*I Kings* 11:29-39); (2) he announces the death of Jeroboam's little son, the end of Jeroboam's dynasty, and the Assyrian captivity of North Israel when Jeroboam's wife comes to him in disguise (14:5-16). Likewise the prophet Shemaiah is important in two events concerning Rehoboam: (1) he charges Rehoboam not to go to war against Jeroboam when the North Israelites murder Adoram (12:21-24); (2) he tells Rehoboam that God is planning to destroy Jerusalem by the Egyptian army under Shishak, and Rehoboam and his comrades humble themselves so that the city is spared (*II Chronicles* 12:5-12).

REVIEW QUESTIONS

1. Enumerate some of the seeds of division that were being sown in Israel before the division of the kingdom during the days of Jeroboam and Rehoboam. What lesson can the church learn from this? Discuss.

2. What did Rehoboam do to cause the division between Israel and Judah? *I Kings* 12:11-14. What did the Israelites do to cause this division? 12:18. Discuss how these two principles can cause strife and contention in the home and in the church.

3. In what four specific ways did Jeroboam lead North Israel into apostasy from God? *I Kings* 12:28-33. What can the contemporary believer and church learn from this? In what ways did Rehoboam fall away from God? *I Kings* 14:23-24; *II Chronicles* 11:21; 12:1. What can the believer and the church learn from this? Discuss these two kinds of apostasy at length.

4. Relate the story of the prophet of Judah and the old prophet of Bethel. *I Kings* 13:7-34. What was the difficult decision with which the prophet of Judah was faced? How did he deal with it? Was he dishonest? Was he innocent? Discuss. What lesson can modern man learn from this?

5. How was Jeroboam punished for leading North Israel into apostasy? *I Kings* 14:1-20. How was Rehoboam punished for abandoning the Lord? 14:25-29. What fundamental lesson is taught here? Discuss.

6. State and discuss the two events in the life of Jeroboam in which the prophet Ahijah was involved, and the two events in the life of Rehoboam in which the prophet Shemaiah was involved. *I Kings* 11:29-29; 14:5-16; 12:21-24; *II Chronicles* 12:5-12. What important lessons concerning the role of a true prophet in Israelite and Judean life can be learned from this?

7. What prediction did the prophet of Judah make concerning the altar that Jeroboam had made at Bethel? *I Kings* 13:2. When and by whom was this prediction fulfilled? *II Kings* 23:15-16; see 22:3. How much time expired between the prediction and its fulfillment? How can this help one believe more fully in the inspiration of the men of God who spoke and wrote inspired truth? Discuss.

Lesson II

FROM BELIEF TO UNBELIEF—
THE STORY OF ASA KING OF JUDAH
(I KINGS 15:1-16:14; II CHRONICLES 13-16)

"You were running well; who hindered you from obeying the truth?" (Galatians 5:7)

The Bible gives very little information concerning most of the kings of Israel and Judah. The main characters are the prophets. The lessons in this booklet, therefore, give primary attention to those kings and prophets who were most significant in the spiritual life of these two kingdoms. This lesson deals mainly with Asa and three prophets associated with him (directly or indirectly): Jehu, Azariah, and Hanani. But first, brief attention must be given to other kings of Israel and Judah who reigned near the time of Asa.

Three Kings of Israel—Nadab, Baasha, and Elah (I Kings 15:25-16:14)

Nadab the son of Jeroboam I reigns over Israel parts of two years (901-900 B. C.). While he is attacking the Philistine city of Gibbethon (probably the modern Tell el-Melat about 3 miles west of Gezer), a portion of his army led by Baasha of the tribe of Issachar rebels against him, and Baasha kills him. Baasha proceeds to kill all the house of Jeroboam I, thus bringing the dynasty of Jeroboam to an abrupt end, as the prophet Ahijah had predicted (*I Kings* 15:25-32).

Baasha begins the second North Israelite dynasty. He reigns over Israel at Tirzah (the modern Tell el-Far'ah about 7 miles east of Samaria and 7 miles north-northeast of Shechem) for 24 years (900-877 B. C.). He is defeated by Asa of Judah and Ben-hadad I (ca. 885-870 B. C.) of Syria

10

when he tries to cut off Asa from communication with other nations (*II Chronicles* 16:1-6; the details are given below under the discussion of Asa). Because of his wickedness, God sends the prophet Jehu to him to announce that his dynasty would be swept away just like that of Jeroboam I (*I Kings* 15:33-16:7).

Elah the son of Baasha reigns over Israel at Tirzah for parts of two years (877-876 B. C.). Zimri, the commander of half of his chariots, rebels against him and kills him at Tirzah while he is drunk. Then Zimri slays all the house of Baasha, as the prophet Jehu had predicted (16:8-14).

Abijah and Judah's Victory over Jeroboam I (I Kings 15:1-8; II Chronicles 13)

While Jeroboam I is still ruling North Israel, Rehoboam dies and is succeeded by his son Abijah (Kings—Abijam), who reigns three years (915-913 B. C.) in Jerusalem. Abijah's heart is "not wholly true to the Lord" as was David's, but he follows in the footsteps of his father Rehoboam. Among other things, he has 14 wives (*II Chronicles* 13:21). However, for David's sake, God does not allow him to be destroyed (*I Kings* 15:1-8).

Abijah and Jeroboam go to war with one another at Mount Zemaraim (located somewhere in the hill country of Ephraim). Abijah chides Jeroboam for dividing the Israelites into two nations, making the two golden calves at Dan and Bethel, and driving out the descendants of Levi as priests and consecrating people from all tribes as priests. He urges him not to fight against the Judeans, because God is at their head leading them, and they have Levitical priests serving him. Jeroboam tries to ambush Abijah's forces, but they cry out to the Lord and he defeats Jeroboam and gives the Israelite soldiers into their hand. Outnumbered two to one (see *II Chronicles* 13:3), Abijah and the Judeans are victorious because they "rely" on the Lord (13:18). As a result of this victory, Judah controls certain North Israelite cities for a time (*II Chronicles* 13).

Asa King of Judah and His Diminishing Faith (I Kings 15:9-24; II Chronicles 14-16)

Like Saul, David, and Solomon, Asa begins his reign with

great faith in God, but as time goes on he manifests less trust in the Lord and more trust in human power, to his own discredit and shame. The Bible describes four major events connected with Asa, the first two demonstrating his belief in God, and the last two his lack of trust.

First, early in his reign Asa carries out a rather far-reaching reform which was necessitated by the apostasies perpetrated by Solomon, Rehoboam, and Abijah. Asa removes the male cult prostitutes, idols, and foreign altars which these kings had brought into the land, and he urges the people to seek the Lord and keep his law. The Lord blesses him by giving him peace for 10 years, during which time he builds fortified cities and increases his army and their weapons (*I Kings* 15:9-12; *II Chronicles* 14:1-8).

Second, Zerah the Ethiopian brings a large army against Asa at Mareshah (the modern Tell Sandahannah ca. 20 south-west of Jerusalem). Asa realizes that by their own strength the Judeans cannot resist Zerah's attack, so he calls upon God to fight for Judah and declares that he and his people "rely" on him (*II Chronicles* 14:11). The Lord intervenes and defeats the Ethiopians, and the Judeans take great spoil. As Asa returns from the battle, God sends the prophet Azariah to him to encourage him to continue to seek the Lord rather than human strength. This stimulates Asa to carry his reform farther. He puts away foreign idols from the land, repairs the altar at the Jerusalem temple, gathers both Judeans and North Israelites to Jerusalem to enter into a covenant with the Lord to seek him "with all their heart and with all their soul," removes his own mother from being queen mother because she had made an image for Asherah and destroys her image, and brings rich gifts into the temple treasury (*I Kings* 15:13-15; *II Chronicles* 14:9-15:19). It looks as if Asa's faith in God is strong and increasing, and then another crisis arises.

Third, Baasha the king of Israel decides to fortify Ramah to cut off all communication and commerce from Asa. Instead of trusting in God (as he had done when Zerah attacked), Asa sends large amounts of silver and gold from the treasuries of the temple and the king's palace to Ben-hadad I king of Syria to make a league with him to go to war against Baasha. Ben-hadad gladly accepts the offer, brings the Syrian army against the Israelites and conquers several of their cities so that Baasha is forced to abandon his building program at Ramah. God sends the prophet Hanani to Asa to rebuke him for "relying" on Ben-hadad rather than on God (*II Chronicles* 16:7-8). The Lord had delivered him from Zerah and would have delivered him from Baasha if he had only trusted in him. Hanani tells Asa, "You have done foolishly in this" (16:9). This calls to mind Samuel's statement to Saul when he did not wait for him seven days at Gilgal before offering the burnt offering (*I Samuel* 13:13), and Tamar's reply to Amnon when he asked her to commit fornication with him (*II Samuel* 13:12). Asa becomes very angry at Hanani and puts him in stocks in prison (*I Kings* 15:16-22; *II Chronicles* 16:1-10).

Fourth, toward the end of his reign Asa becomes severely diseased in his feet. But instead of praying to God for help and trusting in him, Asa seeks help from the physicians (*I Kings* 15:23-24; *II Chronicles* 16:11-14), who undoubtedly had little scientific medical knowledge and were more like magicians or fortune-tellers (one calls to mind the incident involving Saul and the medium of Endor, *I Samuel* 28:3-25). But even when one goes to a well-trained doctor, he must trust in the Lord and not in man's skills or knowledge, because, while man may participate in the healing process it is God alone who can heal the sick.

God's Prophets
It is important to keep in mind that the main characters in the events described in these chapters are not the kings, but the prophets. The prophet Jehu condemns Baasha for his sins, and announces the end of his dynasty (*I Kings* 16:1-7). Azariah encourages Asa to continue to trust in God after the king had relied on him when Judah was attacked by Zerah and the Ethiopians, and this inspires Asa to expand the reform he had begun earlier (*II Chronicles* 15). Hanani condemns Asa because he relies on Ben-Hadad of Syria rather than on the Lord to help him in his struggle with Baasha, and the king puts him in prison (16:7-10).

REVIEW QUESTIONS

1. Relate briefly the vital details concerning the reigns of the North Israelite kings Nadab, Baasha, and Elah. *I Kings* 15:25-16:14. Name the first two North Israelite dynasties, tell who predicted the end of each, and tell how each came to an end.

2. Tell of the war between Abijah and Jeroboam. For what three sins did Abijah rebuke Jeroboam? Who won the war? Why? *II Chronicles* 13. Discuss the implications of this for Christian living.

3. State and elaborate on two events in Asa's career in which he manifested his faith in God. *I Kings* 15:9-15; *II Chronicles* 14-15. Who was the prophet that encouraged Asa to continue trusting in God? What did his encouragement motivate Asa to do?

4. Relate two events in Asa's reign in which he displayed a lack of trust in God. *I Kings* 15-16-24; *II Chronicles* 16. Who was the prophet that condemned his lack of faith? What can the Christian learn from the spiritual life of Asa? Discuss at length.

5. Who was the prophet that condemned Baasha for his sins? What did he predict concerning Baasha? *I Kings* 16:1-7. With what is this similar in a previous king's life and reign?

6. Who were the two prophets that figured into Asa's career? What role did each play? *II Chronicles* 15; 16:1-7. Discuss the importance of the prophets in the religious life of Israel and Judah in light of these events.

Lesson III

GOD'S PEOPLE BECOME VERY CORRUPT—
THE DYNASTY OF OMRI
(I KINGS 16:15-II KINGS 2:11;
II CHRONICLES 18)

"You shall sow, but not reap;
you shall tread olives, but not anoint yourselves with oil;
you shall tread grapes, but not drink wine.
For you have kept the statutes of Omri,
and all the works of the house of Ahab;
and you have walked in their counsels." (Micah 6:15-16)

The careers and work of the North Israelite prophets Elijah and Elisha took place during the days of the third dynasty in that territory (after that of Jeroboam I and of Baasha)—the Dynasty of Omri. This lesson gives a brief sketch of the reigns of the kings belonging to that dynasty; then Lesson IV will deal with Elijah, and Lesson V with Elisha.

Omri (876-869 B. C.)

Zimri, who killed Elah and the other sons of Baasha and thus brought the dynasty of Baasha to an end, reigns only seven days over Israel in Tirzah (876 B. C.). The Israelite army is again besieging the Philistine city of Gibbethon (as they had done in the days of Baasha, see 15:27), when they learn that Zimri had murdered Elah. They immediately make Omri their king, leave Gibbethon, and besiege Tirzah. Zimri is very fearful and commits suicide by burning down the king's house around him. Israel is divided between Omri and Tibni, but probably after a struggle that lasts about four years, the followers of Omri prevail and he is made king. The famous

Moabite Stone of Mesha king of Moab states that Omri overran Northern Moab and that it was subject to Israel for 40 years (lines 4-8). Omri purchases the hill of Samaria from Shemer, fortifies it with a strong wall and towers, and calls it "Samaria" after Shemer. From the time of Omri, Samaria is the capital of North Israel (*I Kings* 16:15-28). Omri was undoubtedly a powerful king, because Assyrian records refer to Samaria as the "House of Omri," and to the land of Israel as the "land of Omri." The Black Obelisk of Shalmaneser III of Assyria (842 B. C.) refers to Jehu (who is not related to the Omri dynasty) as the "son of Omri."

Ahab (869-850 B. C.)

Ahab the son of Omri succeeds his father on the throne of North Israel in Samaria. Evidently as a political maneuver to strengthen his power against Syria, he marries Jezebel the daughter of Ethbaal (Ittobaal) king of the Sidonians (in Phoenicia) and priest of the goddess Astarte. To please his wife, he builds a temple and an altar to Baal in Samaria, and serves and worships him, and makes an Asherah (*I Kings* 16:29-33). He increases the military strength of Israel by building several fortified cities (*I Kings* 22:39). In his days, Hiel of Bethel rebuilds Jericho, which the Israelites under Joshua had destroyed (*Joshua* 6:1-21). During this building program, two of Hiel's sons die (*I Kings* 16:34), thus fulfilling Joshua's predictive curse (*Joshua* 6:26). Archeologists have discovered large numbers of carved ivory pieces dating from the time of Ahab, which fits the reference to Ahab's "ivory house" (*I Kings* 22:39).

There is constant war between Israel and Syria in the days of Ahab. The Old Testament preserves records of three of these. (a) Ben-hadad I, the king of Syria (880-842 B. C.), besieges Samaria, and charges Ahab to give him his wives and children, gold and silver, and to let his servants take whatever they please of Ahab's treasures. Ahab refuses, and Ben-hadad threatens to rout the city. Ahab sends him this message: "Let not him that girds on his armor boast himself as he that puts it off" (*I Kings* 20:11). It is not as easy to accomplish a task or to win a victory as one might think or claim. A prophet tells Ahab that the Lord will give him the victory that he might know that Yahweh (and not Baal) is God (*I Kings* 20:13), and the Israelites soundly defeat the Syrians (20:1-21).

16

(b) The servants of Ben-hadad tell him that the reason they lost the battle is that Yahweh is a god of the hills while the Syrian god is a god of the plains. Convinced that the Syrians can overcome the Israelites, in the Spring of the next year Ben-hadad leads his army against Aphek. A prophet tells Ahab that the Lord will give him the victory that he may know that Yahweh (and not Baal) is God (20:28). Israel wins the battle, spares Ben-hadad's life in return for the cities which Ben-hadad's father had taken from Ahab's father, and Ahab and Ben-hadad make a peaceful covenant. A prophet has one of his fellows to strike him so that it will appear that he has been attacked. He disguises himself as a wounded soldier and meets Ahab as he comes by. He declares that a Syrian soldier had been left in his custody, and while he was occupied with other things this soldier struck him and escaped. Ahab condemns the prophet; but the prophet quickly removes his disguise and rebukes the king for allowing Ben-hadad to escape from him at Aphek when he should have killed him. So, the judgment he had declared on the prophet is self-condemning, just as was the judgment of David on the rich man of Nathan's parable (*II Samuel* 12:1-7). The prophet announces that Ben-hadad will be responsible for Ahab's death (20:22-43). The covenant between Ahab and Ben-hadad comes at a very advantageous time, according to the inscription of Shalmaneser III, because in 853 B. C. he brought his powerful Assyrian army against Qarqar (about 45 miles north-northwest of Hamath) in Syria. Ahab of Israel, Ben-hadad of Damascus, Irhuleni of Hamath, and other kings in the region fight valiantly and apparently hold Assyria to a stalemate, in spite of Shalmaneser's claim (preserved on his inscription) that the Assyrians were victorious.

(c) After three years of peace, Ahab makes a league with Jehoshaphat of Judah to attack Ramoth-gilead (the modern Tell er-Ramith ca. 25 miles east of the northern reaches of the Jordan a few miles south of the Sea of Galilee) in an effort to reclaim it for Israel out of the hands of Ben-hadad and Syria. Jehoshaphat insists on inquiring of the Lord before they leave for battle. Ahab summons Zedekiah and 400 prophets (of Baal?), who declare that Israel and Judah will defeat Syria, but Jehoshaphat is not satisfied. He asks if there is not another prophet of the Lord of whom they might inquire. Ahab replies, "There is yet one man by whom we may inquire of the Lord, Micaiah the son of Imlah; but I hate him, for he never prophesies good concerning me, but evil" (22:8). Jehoshaphat wishes to hear him, so Ahab sends a messenger to Micaiah, who urges him to encourage the two kings to go up and fight against Syria at Ramoth-gilead. Micaiah mockingly gives this reply at first, but when Ahab rebukes him for not telling the truth, Micaiah states that the Lord's will is that they not fight in this battle since they have no reputable "shepherd" or "master" to lead them. When Ahab reacts negatively, Micaiah relates a vision. The Lord was sitting on his throne with all the host of heaven standing about him. He asks the heavenly beings, "Who will entice Ahab, that he may go up and fall at Ramoth-gilead?" (22:20). One spirit says that he will do it by becoming a lying spirit in the mouth of all Ahab's prophets. The Lord tells him to go. Upon hearing this, Ahab has Micaiah imprisoned. When the battle of Ramoth-gilead begins, Ahab disguises himself, but a Syrian archer shoots him with an arrow without realizing who he is, and Ahab dies, thus fulfilling the prediction of the prophet who disguised himself and spoke to him on the road (20:42), and that of Micaiah. The Israelite soldiers return Ahab's body to Samaria in his chariot, and he is buried there. They wash his chariot by the pool of Samaria, and dogs lick his blood which has collected in the bottom of the chariot, thus fulfilling Elijah's prediction that he would be killed for the murder of Naboth, and that dogs would lick his blood in the same place they had licked Naboth's (21:19) (22:1-40; *II Chronicles* 18).

Ahaziah (850-849 B. C.)

Ahab is succeeded by his son Ahaziah, who, like his father, is not faithful to the Lord, but worships Baal-zebub the god of the Philistine city of Ekron (*I Kings* 22:51-53; *II Kings* 1:2). Jehoshaphat king of Judah joins Ahaziah in building ships at Ezion-geber to go to Tarshish (which calls to mind Solomon's league with Hiram, *I Kings* 10:22), but Eliezer the prophet condemns Jehoshaphat for entering into a league with such a wicked king, and the Lord causes the ships to be wrecked so that they cannot go (*II Chronicles* 20:35-37). A short time later, Ahaziah proposes to Jehoshaphat that they attempt to go on ships of Tarshish to Ophir to get gold, but this time Jehoshaphat refuses (*I Kings* 22:47-50). After reigning only parts of two years, Ahaziah falls through a window in the upper chamber of his palace in Samaria, and sends messengers to inquire of Baal-zebub the god of Ekron whether he will survive. Elijah apprehends them and declares that Ahaziah will die; it comes to pass (*II Kings* 1).

Jehoram (849-842 B. C.)

As Ahaziah has no son, he is succeeded by his brother (another son of Ahab) Jehoram. Although Jehoram puts away the pillar of Baal that Ahab had made (see *I Kings* 16:31-32), he continues to follow the apostate practices instituted by Jeroboam I (described in 12:28-33). When Ahab died ca. 850 B. C., Mesha the king of Moab rebelled against Israel (*II Kings* 1:1; 3:5), which had ruled over Moab since the days of Omri (according to the Moabite Stone, lines 4-8). Apparently Ahaziah made no attempt to overcome this rebellion. However, Jehoram makes a league with Jehoshaphat of Judah and the king of Edom to attack Moab and bring it back under Israelite control. In keeping with a prediction of the prophet Elisha (3:18-19), they defeat Moab handily (for details, see Lesson V).

Several battles between Israel and Syria take place during the reign of Jehoram, representing a continuation of the same circumstances that existed in the days of Ahab. *II Kings* 5:2 refers to Syrian "raids" against Israel, and verse 7 indicates that Jehoram thought that Ben-hadad I's letter to him asking him to heal Naaman of his leprosy was a calculated attempt to draw Israel into another war. Elisha saves Jehoram's life several times by telling him where Ben-hadad intends to attack next. This angers Ben-hadad, and he surrounds the city of Dothan (the modern Tell Dotha ca. 16 miles north-northwest of Shechem) where Elisha is staying. The Lord smites the Syrian soldiers with blindness and Elisha leads them into Samaria, where Jehoram gives them food and drink and releases them at the command of Elisha (6:8-23). On another occasion, Ben-hadad besieges Samaria. The food and water supply is cut off, so that there is a great famine in the city. Elisha declares that the city will be delivered shortly. The next morning four lepers discover that during the night the Syrians had fled, and the people of Samaria take the Syrian spoil (6:24-7:20). Elisha tells Hazael that he will follow Ben-hadad as king over Damascus. Hazael smothers

Ben-hadad to death in his bed, and seizes the throne (842-798 B. C.) (8:7-15). Jehoram makes a league with Ahaziah of Judah to make another attempt to regain Ramoth-gilead from Syria (Ahab and Jehoshaphat had attempted this and failed, see *I Kings* 22:1-38). The Syrians wound Jehoram and he returns to Jezreel to recover. While he is there, Jehu attacks the city and kills Jehoram, thus ending the powerful Omri dynasty in North Israel. Jehu has Jehoram's body cast on the plot of ground that had belonged to Naboth as retribution for Naboth's blood which Ahab had shed to secure his vineyard (*II Kings* 8:28-29; 9:14-26).

The Prophets Connected With the Omri Dynasty

As the events described above make clear, there are at least five prophets directly or indirectly connected with the kings of the Omri dynasty. (1) When Ahab releases Ben-hadad at Aphek, an unnamed prophet meets him disguised as a soldier who had allowed a Syrian prisoner to escape. When Ahab condemns him for this, he condemns Ahab for allowing the king of Syria to go free (*I Kings* 20:26-43). (2) Micaiah urges Ahab and Jehoshaphat not to fight against Ben-hadad at Ramoth-gilead, for if they do Ahab will be killed in the battle. They refuse Micaiah's advice, and Ahab is killed (22:1-38). (3) Eliezer rebukes Jehoshaphat of Judah for making a league with Ahaziah of Israel to build ships at Ezion-geber to go to Tarshish, and the ships are broken so that they cannot go (*II Chronicles* 20:35-37). (4) Elijah constantly condemns Ahab and Ahaziah for their infidelity to God (Lesson IV). (5) Elisha works diligently during the reign of Jehoram to try to bring the king and the people back to God (Lesson V).

REVIEW QUESTIONS

1. Tell how Zimri died, and relate the struggle for power in North Israel after his death. Who won this struggle and became king? Where did he make a new capital? Where had the capital of Israel been before this? *I Kings* 16:15-28. What is the source of our information that this king overran Moab? Read this source in J. B. Pritchard's *Ancient Near Eastern Texts* or D. W. Thomas's *Documents from Old Testament Times,* and discuss it at length.

2. Whom did Ahab marry? What was her background? What did Ahab build in Samaria to please her? *I Kings* 16:29-33. What lesson can the contemporary Christian learn from this about marrying someone who is not a Christian? Discuss.

3. Who rebuilt the city of Jericho which Joshua had destroyed? What losses did he incur in the process? *I Kings* 16:34. Who had predicted that this would happen? *Joshua* 6:26. How long was it between this prediction and its fulfillment? (Do your own computing on this by using good books on Old Testament history dealing with the dates of Joshua and Ahab). How does this aid one in building confidence in the guidance of God in the lives of his people and in the inspiration of the Bible? Discuss.

4. Tell of three wars between Ahab and Ben-hadad I of Syria described in the Old Testament. *I Kings* 20:1-21, 22-43; 22:1-38. According to an Assyrian inscription, Ahab and Ben-hadad joined forces against Assyria in another battle. Tell where this battle was fought, against whom, and when. Who won this battle? Do additional research on this, and share the results of this research with the class.

5. Relate the story of Micaiah the prophet. What was the vision that he told Ahab and Jehoshaphat? *I Kings* 22:1-38. Discuss.

6. With whom did Ahaziah of Israel make a league to build ships at Ezion-geber to go to Tarshish for trade on the high seas? Who condemned this king for making a league with Ahaziah? Why? What happened to the ships? *II Chronicles* 20:35-37. How did this king respond the second time Ahaziah proposed that they ally in a commercial project involving travel by ship? *I Kings* 22:47-50.

7. Tell of the battles that took place between Israel and Syria during the time of Jehoram. Relate the ways the prophet Elisha figures into these events. *II Kings* 5:2, 7; 6:8-23; 6:24-7:20; 8:7-15. How did Jehoram die? 8:28-29; 9:14-26. Whose dynasty did this bring to an end? List the three dynasties that have now ruled over Israel.

Lesson IV

A MAN WHO DARED TO STAND ALONE—
THE PROPHET ELIJAH
(I KINGS 17-19, 21; II KINGS 1:1-2:11)

"The Lord is my light and my salvation;
whom shall I fear?
The Lord is the stronghold of my life;
of whom shall I be afraid?" (Psalm 27:1)

The prophet Elijah was from Tishbe (*I Kings* 17:1; 21:17, 28; *II Kings* 1:3, 8; 9:36; exact location unknown) in Gilead east of Jordan, and thus was a native of North Israel. His prophetic career occurred primarily in the reigns of Ahab (869-850 B. C.) and Ahaziah (850-849 B. C.) of the dynasty of Omri (see Lesson III). The Bible records eleven events in his life, which are the subject of this lesson. These events point to three major emphases in Elijah's life and work: (a) a zealous commitment to Yahweh and dependence on him; (b) a strong opposition to Baalism, which Ahab and Jezebel were promoting in North Israel; and (c) a deep concern for the poor and oppressed. In these specifics, he is quite similar to all the true prophets of God.

Elijah prays that it might not rain (I Kings 17:1-7)
Because Ahab marries Jezebel and brings the worship of Baal into North Israel, Elijah prays that it might not rain (*James* 5:17), and when the Lord answers him he announces it to Ahab. The withholding of rain is one way in which God punishes sinners to try to bring them to repentance (see *Deuteronomy* 11:16-17; *I Kings* 8:35; *Amos* 4:7). To escape death at the hand of Ahab, the Lord tells Elijah to hide at the brook Cherith east of Jordan. During the early days of

22

the drought, Elijah is sustained by ravens who bring him meat and bread twice a day and by drinking water out of the brook. But in time the brook runs dry.

Elijah and the Widow of Zarephath (I Kings 17:8-16)

At the Lord's command, Elijah goes to Zarephath (the modern Sarafand ca. 6 miles south of Sidon) in Phoenicia to be fed by a widow. She has only a handful of meal in a jar and a little oil in a cruse, and she is gathering sticks to build a fire to cook this so that she and her son can eat their final meal and die. Elijah tells her that the meal and oil will not fail until the Lord sends rain, and it comes to pass. Jesus uses this incident to emphasize that a prophet can do good, but only to those who receive him (*Luke* 4:25-26).

Elijah Raises the Widow's Son (I Kings 17:17-24)

The son of the widow of Zarephath dies, and the widow blames the tragedy on Elijah. The prophet takes the lad to his room, lays him on his bed, stretches himself on him three times, and prays to the Lord to revive him. The Lord does so, and Elijah restores him to his mother. She declares that she now knows that Elijah is a prophet and speaks the truth.

The Contest between Elijah and Jezebel's Prophets (I Kings 18:1-40)

The Lord sends Elijah to tell Ahab that he would send rain. Ahab and the ruler of his household, Obadiah, are seeking patches of grass to try to save the animals used by the royal court. Elijah meets Obadiah and tells him to inform Ahab of his presence. However, Obadiah is afraid that if he goes to Ahab, Elijah will disappear; then the king will be angry at Obadiah and kill him, because Obadiah had saved the lives of 100 prophets of Yahweh when Jezebel had them slaughtered. Elijah assures Obadiah that he will meet Ahab, so Obadiah goes to get him. When Ahab meets Elijah, he says: "Is it you, you troubler of Israel?" (verse 17), apparently referring to Elijah's prayer that it might not rain. Elijah replies that it was not he who was ultimately responsible for the drought, but Ahab, because the king had forsaken the Lord and followed Baal.

Elijah charges Ahab to gather Israel and the 850 prophets of Jezebel (i. e., 450 prophets of Baal and 400 prophets of

Asherah) to Mount Carmel. When the Israelites arrive, Elijah rebukes them for "limping with two different opinions," i. e., for trying to serve Yahweh and Baal at the same time, and urges them to commit themselves completely to the one or to the other (verse 21). One is reminded of Jesus' statement, "No one can serve two masters: for either he will hate the one and love the other, or he will be devoted to the one and despise the other. You cannot serve God and mammon (i. e., money)" (*Matthew* 6:24). Elijah then invites Jezebel's prophets to prepare a sacrifice, and states that if Baal answers by consuming it with fire, then it must be admitted that Baal is God. They prepare the sacrifice, call on Baal to answer by fire, limp about the altar, cry aloud, and cut themselves until the blood gushes out, but there is no response from Baal. During this time (from morning till evening), Elijah mocks Jezebel's prophets by suggesting sarcastically four reasons why Baal does not answer. (1) Perhaps he is in deep thought. (2) Possibly he has gotten lost. (3) Maybe he is on a trip. (4) He might be asleep. These ironical statements incite these prophets to try harder, but to no avail.

When evening comes, Elijah repairs the altar of the Lord that had been thrown down (apparently by Ahab and Jezebel) by taking 12 stones (one for each of the 12 tribes of Israel) and building it. He places a sacrifice upon it, and has water poured in the trench so that it cannot be said that he started the fire by some trick. Then he prays that Yahweh will consume the sacrifice. The fire of the Lord consumes the burnt offering, and the people affirm that Yahweh is God. Then Elijah kills the 850 prophets of Jezebel at the brook Kishon (which flows from Mount Carmel southeastward through the Plain of Jezreel).

Elijah prays for rain (I Kings 18:41-46)
Elijah tells Ahab that it will soon rain. Then he goes to the top of Mount Carmel and prays fervently for rain (see *James* 5:18). He sends his servant to the Mediterranean coast seven times to view the weather situation; when he returns the seventh time, he tells Elijah that he had seen a cloud about the size of a man's fist. Elijah tells Ahab to ride his chariot quickly to Jezreel lest the rain stop him, and Elijah runs before him to the entrance of Jezreel.

24

Elijah asks the Lord to take his life (I Kings 19:1-8)

When Ahab tells Jezebel that Elijah had killed her prophets, she sends him a message stating that she would kill him immediately. In fear, Elijah flees south to Beer-sheba, sits down under a broom tree, and asks the Lord to let him die. While he is asleep, an angel awakens him twice to eat a cake and drink some water for a journey. This food gives him enough strength for 40 days and 40 nights to go much farther south to Mount Horeb (i. e., Sinai).

The Lord appears to Elijah at Mount Horeb (I Kings 19:9-18)

Elijah stays in a cave at Mount Horeb. The Lord comes to him and asks him what he is doing. Elijah replies that he had been very jealous for the Lord, because the Israelites had forsaken him and Elijah was the only true prophet left, and Ahab and Jezebel were seeking his life (verse 10). The Lord passes by Elijah in "a great and strong wind," "an earthquake," and "a fire," but the Lord is in none of these. Then he comes to the prophet in "a still small voice," asking him what he is doing. Again Elijah proclaims his jealousy for the Lord (verse 14). The Lord tells him to anoint Hazael king of Syria in place of Ben-hadad I, Jehu king of Israel, and Elisha to replace him as prophet, in order to destroy the worshippers of Baal. Then he announces that he would leave 7000 people in Israel who had not worshipped Baal (verse 18). It is very easy for a zealous worker for the Lord to believe that he alone is fully committed to the Lord. But there are thousands who quietly serve him diligently every day without public acknowledgment or praise, who are just as committed as the well-known servants of God (see *Romans* 11:1-6).

Elijah selects Elisha as his Successor (I Kings 19:19-21)

Elijah finds Elisha plowing with 12 yoke of oxen. He casts his mantle over Elisha, evidently signifying that he had chosen him to succeed him as prophet (see verse 16). Elisha says farewell to his father and mother, and becomes Elijah's minister.

Elijah condemns Ahab for the Murder of Naboth (I Kings 21)

A man of Jezreel named Naboth has a vineyard joining the property on which Ahab's palace was located at Jezreel. Ahab offers Naboth to buy or trade for his vineyard, but Naboth refuses because the land is his family's inheritance.

Ahab returns to his palace, lies down on his bed, turns away his face pouting, and refuses to eat. When Jezebel learns what has happened, she sends letters with Ahab's seal upon them, instructing the elders and nobles of Jezreel to set up two base fellows to charge Naboth with cursing God and the king. They do so, and Naboth is stoned to death for his alleged crime.

When Ahab learns that Naboth is dead, he goes to Jezreel to take possession of his vineyard. But the Lord sends Elijah to apprehend him, and to announce that where the dogs licked up the blood of Naboth they would lick up the king's blood. Ahab replies, "Have you found me, O my enemy?" And Elijah responds, "I have found you, because you have sold yourself to do what is evil in the sight of the Lord" (verse 20). He declares that the Lord will bring the dynasty of Omri to an end, just as he had done to the dynasties of Jeroboam I and Baasha (verse 22). He also announces that the dogs would lick up the blood of Jezebel in Jezreel. Elijah's severe statements cause Ahab to humble himself, and the Lord declares that he will not bring these punishments on Omri's house in Ahab's lifetime.

Elijah and the Illness of Ahaziah (II Kings 1)
Ahab's son, Ahaziah, falls through a window in the upper chamber of the royal palace in Samaria and is very ill. He sends messengers to inquire of Baal-zebub, the god of Ekron. The Lord sends Elijah to apprehend these messengers and to tell them that Ahaziah would die. Upon learning that it is Elijah who sent this message, Ahaziah sends two groups of 50 soldiers each to bring Elijah to him, but each time Elijah prays the Lord to send fire from heaven to consume them. The captain of the third group of 50 pleads with Elijah to go with him, and he does. He announces to Ahaziah that he would die, and this comes to pass.

Elijah is Taken Up to Heaven (II Kings 2:1-11)
Near the end of Elijah's career, he and Elisha go together from Gilgal to Bethel to Jericho to the Jordan. Elijah strikes the water of the Jordan with his mantle and it parts, so that the two prophets can cross over on dry ground. Elijah asks Elisha what he can do for him before he is taken away, and Elisha asks him for a double portion of his spirit. Elijah says

that if Elisha sees him taken up, he will be granted this request. A chariot of fire and horses separate the two men, and Elijah is taken up by a whirlwind into heaven. This incident calls to mind Enoch's transport into heaven (*Genesis* 5:24; *Hebrews* 11:5). It may be that this was the original means God intended to carry man off the earth to live in eternity rather than by death. In keeping with this, it is interesting that Paul teaches that those who are alive when Christ returns will be changed in a moment and will be caught up to meet him in the air (see *I Thessalonians* 4:13-18; *I Corinthians* 15:50-57). At any rate, there is no indication in the Bible that God ever intended for the earth to be man's eternal home.

REVIEW QUESTIONS

1. Under what two kings did Elijah do his prophetic work? What are the approximate dates of their reigns? What three major emphases can one deduce from studying the events in Elijah's life? Are these emphases relevant to Christian concerns today? Discuss.

2. Why did Elijah pray that it might not rain? *I Kings* 16:30-17:1. See *James* 5:17. How was Elijah sustained during the early days of the famine? *I Kings* 17:2-7. When the brook Cherith ran dry, where did God send him for sustenance? 17:8-16. Describe the way in which Elijah was able to survive in this new circumstance.

3. Relate the story of Elijah raising the widow's son from the dead. *I Kings* 17:17-24. On the basis of your own research, name some other incidents in the Old Testament in which someone was raised from the dead. How is Jesus' resurrection unique? Discuss.

4. What two terms does Ahab use to describe Elijah? *I Kings* 18:17; 21:20. How does Elijah answer him in each case? What practical lesson can one learn from this for modern Christian thinking and living?

5. Relate the story of the contest between Elijah and the prophets of Jezebel. *I Kings* 18:19-40. For what four reasons did Elijah mockingly suggest to these prophets that Baal was not answering them? 18:27. What did the prophets of Jezebel do to try to encourage Baal to respond to them? 18:26, 28. What did Elijah do to these prophets? 18:40.

6. When the Lord asked Elijah what he was doing in the cave at Mount Horeb (Sinai), what did Elijah say? *I Kings* 19:10, 14. In what did the Lord appear to Elijah? 19:12. What three persons did God instruct Elijah to anoint? What role was each to play as a result of this anointing? 19:15.

7. What request did Ahab make of Naboth? What was Naboth's response? *I Kings* 21:1-3. How did Ahab respond to this? 21:4. What did Jezebel do to help Ahab get his way? 21:5-16. What did Elijah tell Ahab when he came to take possession of Naboth's vineyard? 21:21-24.

8. Relate the story of Elijah's being taken into heaven. *II Kings* 2:1-11. What request did Elisha make of Elijah before he was taken up? 2:9.

9. Briefly summarize the eleven events involving the prophet Elijah recorded in the Bible. Discuss his life, actions, and teachings with the view of making practical applications to modern day Christian living.

Lesson V

A MAN OF GREAT RELIGIOUS AND ETHICAL STRENGTH– THE PROPHET ELISHA (II KINGS 2:1-8:15; 9:1-10)

"Fear not, for those who are with us are more than those who are with them"
(II Kings 6:16)

The prophet Elisha was from Abel-meholah (*I Kings* 19:16) (which is probably to be identified with Tell el-Maqlub on the Wadi-Yabis east of Jordan, although this is debated). He was a North Israelite prophet whose career fell within the reign of Jehoram of Israel (849-842 B. C., see Lesson III), a son of Ahab. This was a period of insecurity in Israel. Relations with Phoenicia were still strong because of the continued influence of Jezebel, but this meant that large numbers of Israelites were worshipping Baal and living ungodly lives that resulted from that religion. Jehoram had to face a strong rebellion by Mesha king of Moab, and was involved in continuous wars with Syria. From Elisha's deeds and words, it is clear that he had great faith in God in most difficult times, that he strongly opposed the worship of Baal, and that he was concerned to help the poor and needy and oppressed. The Old Testament records seventeen events in the life of Elisha. Two of these (Elijah's call of Elisha, *I Kings* 19:19-21; and Elisha's accompanying Elijah prior to his being taken into heaven, *II Kings* 2:1-11) were discussed in Lesson IV and thus receive only brief attention here.

Elisha Receives Elijah's Mantle (II Kings 2:1-18)
At the Lord's command, Elijah had cast his mantle on Elisha while he was plowing in the field, and he had become Elijah's companion and minister (*I Kings* 19:19-21). So, when the time comes for Elijah to be caught up into heaven,

it is natural that Elisha accompany him (*II Kings* 2:1-11). Just before Elijah is caught up, Elisha asks to receive a double share of this spirit (2:9). As Elijah is caught up, his mantle falls from him. Elisha takes it with him to the Jordan and strikes the water with it, the water parts (as it had done when Elijah struck the water with it, 2:8), and he goes over on dry land. The fifty prophets at Jericho plead with Elisha to let them go look for Elijah. He knows this is futile, but finally allows it because of their urgency. They are unable to find him.

Elisha purifies the Water of Jericho (II Kings 2:19-22)
The men of Jericho complain to Elisha that the water is bad. He puts salt in a new bowl and throws it into the spring. The water becomes wholesome.

Elisha and the 42 boys of Bethel (II Kings 2:23-25)
Elisha goes from Jericho to Bethel. On the way, 42 small boys meet him and speak very disrespectfully of him, saying, "Go up, you baldhead!" He curses them in the name of the Lord, and two she-bears come out of the woods and tear the boys.

Elisha and Jehoram's War against Mesha King of Moab (II Kings 3)
Moab had been subject to Israel during the reigns of Omri and Ahab (according to the Moabite Stone, see Lesson III), but when Ahab died, Mesha the king of Moab rebelled (1:1; 3:5). After Ahaziah's brief reign, Jehoram takes the throne of Israel and decides to march against Mesha. He is joined by the armies of Judah under Jehoshaphat and of Edom. After seven days of marching toward Moab, however, there is no water, and Jehoshaphat suggests that they inquire of a prophet as to how they should proceed. They go to Elisha, who asks Jehoram why he does not go to the prophets of Baal whom Ahab and Jezebel had established in Israel. But because Jehoshaphat is present, Elisha proclaims the Lord's decree in this matter. He tells the allied armies that the stream-bed will be filled with water and that the Lord will give the Moabites into their hand. The water comes the next morning, and when the Moabites see it, they think it is blood and that the attacking armies had killed themselves, so they come down to take spoil. The Israelites kill them. In desperation,

Mesha offers his eldest son as a burnt offering on the wall of Kir-hareseth in Moab, and Jehoram and his allies withdraw.

Elisha helps the Wife of a Prophet pay her debts (II Kings 4:1-7)

The wife of a prophet tells Elisha that her husband is dead and that a creditor has come to take her two children as slaves, since she could not pay him her debts. Elisha tells her to borrow as many vessels as possible from her neighbors, and to fill them with the oil she has in a jar. As long as there are jars, the oil keeps flowing. Elisha tells her to sell it, pay her debts, and live on the money that remains.

Elisha and the birth of a Son to the Woman of Shunem (II Kings 4:8-17)

Elisha frequently stays in the home of a wealthy woman of Shunem (the modern Solem ca. 4 miles north of Jezreel), who lets him stay in a small roof chamber in her home. Elisha asks her how he can repay her for her hospitality, but she makes no request. However, Elisha's servant Gehazi learns that she would like to have a son. Elisha announces to her that she will have a son, and she gives birth to him the following spring.

Elisha Raises the Shunammite Woman's Son from the Dead (II Kings 4:18-37)

One day, when the son of the Shunammite woman is working with his father in the field, he becomes very sick and dies. The woman goes to Elisha. The prophet comes and stretches himself on the lad, and he revives. (This incident calls to mind Elijah raising up the son of the widow of Zarephath, see I Kings 17:17-24).

Elisha cleanses pottage for the Prophets at Gilgal (II Kings 4:38-41)

Elisha comes to Gilgal, where the prophets are boiling pottage. One of them slices wild gourds into it, not knowing what they are. Then the prophets cannot eat it. Elisha throws some meal into the pot, and the prophets are able to eat the pottage.

Elisha Feeds 100 Men (II Kings 4:42-44)

A man of Baal-shalishah brings Elisha 20 loaves of barley

and fresh grain. He multiplies this and feeds 100 men, and there is some left. (This incident calls to mind Jesus' feeding of the 5000 with five barley loaves and two small fish, see *Mark* 6:30-44).

Elisha and Naaman the Leper (II Kings 5)

Naaman, the commander of the Syrian army under Ben-hadad I, is a leper. During a raid on Israel, the Syrians capture a little maid who becomes a servant of Naaman's wife. She tells her mistress that the prophet Elisha in Samaria can cure Naaman. Ben-hadad sends a letter to Jehoram by Naaman, asking him to heal the commander, but Jehoram thinks that Ben-hadad is trying to start another war with him. However, Elisha tells Jehoram to send Naaman to him. When Naaman comes, Elisha sends a messenger to him, telling him to wash in the Jordan seven times and he will be cleansed. Naaman is angered because he wanted Elisha to come to him personally and wave his hand over the place and cure him; he also thinks it would be better to wash in the rivers of Damascus (Abana and Pharpar) rather than in the Jordan. Yet, Naaman's servants persuade him at least to try what Elisha had commanded; and when he does so, he is cleansed (verses 1-14). It is worthy of note that man often thinks that he knows a better way to solve his problems than God does. He views God's way as too simple, or "beneath his dignity." How much better it is to obey God, believing that he knows what is best even when man cannot rationalize it.

Naaman comes to Elisha and admits: "Behold, I know that there is no God in all the earth but in Israel " (verse 15). This is another instance which indicates that in Old Testament times God was concerned that his people try to convert the nations from the worship of false gods to him (see also *Joshua* 4:23-24; *I Samuel* 17:46; *I Kings* 8:60; *Jonah*). Naaman offers Elisha a present, but he refuses. Then the Syrian officer asks for two mules' burden of Israelite soil to take back with him to Damascus, so that he might offer sacrifices to the Lord on that soil. When Naaman departs, Elisha's servant Gehazi follows him, says that two young prophets had come to visit Elisha unexpectedly, and asks Naaman for a talent of silver and two festal garments. Naaman gladly gives him two talents of silver and the garments. When Gehazi returns to Elisha's house, Elisha rebukes him, and tells him that he and his descendants will be stricken with the leprosy of Naaman. Gehazi goes out a leper (verses 15-27). Greed, the lust for wealth, is a powerful temptation of Satan to draw the faithful away from God. Jesus warned: "Take heed, and beware of all covetousness; for a man's life does not consist in the abundance of his possessions" (*Luke* 12:15).

Elisha makes the Axe Head Float (II Kings 6:1-7)

The prophetic band or company (see *I Samuel* 10:5, 10; 19:20) under Elisha suggest that they go to the Jordan to cut down logs, in order that they might build a new building in which to live. While they are working, the head of one of the axes flies off into the water. Elisha cuts off a stick, throws it in the water where the axe head flew off, and makes it float.

Elisha Escapes from the Syrians at Dothan (II Kings 6:8-23)

On several occasions, when Ben-hadad decides to attack Israel at a certain place, Elisha tells Jehoram and saves his life and the lives of his soldiers. Ben-hadad learns that Elisha can forecast his plans to Jehoram, so he sends his soldiers to surround the city of Dothan, where Elisha is staying. Elisha's servant is very perplexed when he learns that the city is surrounded, but Elisha says to him, "Fear not, for those who are with us are more than those who are with them" (6:16). The man who truly trusts in God knows that there is no earthly power that can successfully resist or overcome him (see *Romans* 8:31-39). Such faith can rise above all human fears and doubts. Elisha prays that the Lord strike the Syrians with blindness. Then the prophet leads them to Samaria, has Jehoram prepare a great feast for them, and releases them.

Elisha and the Syrian Siege of Samaria (II Kings 6:24-7:20)

Ben-hadad and his Syrian army besiege Samaria. They cut off the Israelite food supply, food prices are very high in the city, and conditions are very bad. Jehoram learns that people are eating their own children, and he vows to kill Elisha, because he concludes that this attack is the result of Elisha's praying to the Lord, perhaps to punish Israel for her apostasy to Baal. However, Elisha declares that the next day the siege would be lifted and prices would go down. Jehoram's confidant rebukes the prophet for making such a preposterous prediction, and Elisha declares that he will see it happen, but will not eat of the spoil. The next morning four lepers of Samaria decide to risk going to the Syrian camp for food, only to learn that during the night the Syrians had fled. They bring the news back to Samaria, the Israelites seize the spoil, and prices go down in Samaria. The people are so excited about the change of fortune that they trample Jehoram's confidant to death in fulfilment of the word of the Lord through Elisha.

Jehoram restores the Shunammite Woman's Possessions to her (II Kings 8:1-6)

Elisha tells the Shunammite woman to leave Israel because of a severe famine. She goes to Philistia for seven years. When she returns, she goes to Jehoram to ask him to restore her house and land. Just then, Gehazi is telling Jehoram of Elisha's deeds. He recognizes the woman and tells the king, who gladly restores her possessions to her.

Elisha and Hazael of Syria (II Kings 8:7-15)

Ben-hadad I becomes sick in Damascus. He sends Hazael to Elisha (who has come to Damascus) to ask whether he will recover. Elisha tells Hazael to tell Ben-hadad that he will recover, but he tells Hazael that truthfully he will not. Then Elisha weeps because of all the destruction that Hazael will bring upon Israel. Hazael replies, "What is your servant, who is but a dog, that he should do this great thing?" (8:13). The word "dog" is used in a variety of ways to describe various Old Testament characters. It was used of Goliath (*I Samuel* 17:43) and of David (24:14) to connote "insignificance," of Nabal (25:3) to indicate "ill-behavior," of Abner (*II Samuel* 3:8) to suggest "immorality," of Mephibosheth (9:8) to denote "humility," and of Shimei (16:9) to convey "worthlessness." In the case of Hazael, it seems to have reference to his "meanness" in slaughtering the Israelites.

Elisha tells Hazael that the Lord had shown him that he would be king of Syria in place of Ben-hadad. Hazael returns to Ben-hadad and tells him that Elisha said he would recover. But the next day Hazael smothers Ben-hadad to death in his bed, and begins to reign over Syria (841-798 B. C.).

Elisha has Jehu anointed King over Israel (II Kings 9:1-10)

Elisha sends a prophet to Ramoth-gilead to anoint Jehu king over Israel, and to tell him to obliterate the dynasty of Omri ("the house of Ahab") to avenge on Jezebel the blood of God's servants, just as the dynasties of Jeroboam I and Baasha had been eliminated. He announces that the dogs will lick up the blood of Jezebel in Jezreel.

The last two incidents concerning Hazael and Jehu would seem to indicate that the way in which Elijah was to anoint these men kings over their respective nations (see *I Kings* 19:15-17) was through the instrumentality of Elisha after Elijah was taken up into heaven.

REVIEW QUESTIONS

1. Briefly relate the historical and religious conditions which existed in Israel when Elisha did his prophetic work. Tell where Elisha lived as he grew up, who was king over Israel during his prophetic career, and the two events in which he was personally involved with Elijah. *I Kings* 19:16, 19-21; *II Kings* 2:1-11.

2. How did Elisha purify the water of Jericho? *II Kings* 2:19-22. How did he cleanse the pottage at Gilgal? 4:38-41. Discuss any possible parallels between these two incidents.

3. Tell how Elisha helped the prophet's widow pay her debts. *II Kings* 4:1-7.

4. Briefly describe the three events in the life of the Shunammite woman related to Elisha. *II Kings* 4:8-37; 8:1-6. Discuss the similarities and differences between the accounts of Elijah raising the son of the widow of Zarephath from the dead and Elisha raising the Shunammite woman's son from the dead. *I Kings* 17:17-24; *II Kings* 4:18-37.

5. Who was Naaman? How did he learn of Elisha? What did Elisha tell him to do to be cleansed of his leprosy? How did Naaman react to this? *II Kings* 5:1-14. What practical lesson can modern man learn from this? What admission did Naaman make when he was healed? 5:15. What did he take back with him to Damascus? Why? Who followed Naaman after he left Elisha? What request did he make of Naaman? how was he punished for this? 5:16-27. What lesson can the contemporary Christian learn from this? Discuss.

6. Memorize *II Kings* 6:16. Tell briefly the circumstances in which Elisha made this statement. What important lesson does this teach the contemporary disciple of Christ? Discuss.

7. Whom does Elisha make king over Syria? *II Kings* 8:7-15. Whom does he make king over Israel? 9:1-10. How is this to be explained in light of the fact that God had told Elijah to anoint these men kings over their respective nations? *I Kings* 19:15-17. Discuss.

8. Make a list of the seventeen events in the life of Elisha recorded in the Bible. Go over these a number of times so that they will become as familiar as stories concerning Jesus and Paul in the New Testament. Tell these stories to others that they may become more and more familiar.

Lesson VI

RISE IN MATERIALISM; DECLINE IN SPIRITUALITY– THE DYNASTY OF JEHU II KINGS 9-10; 13; 14:7-16, 23-29; 15:8-12)

"Come now, you rich, weep and howl for the miseries that are coming upon you. Your riches have rotted and your garments are moth-eaten. Your gold and silver have rusted, and their rust will be evidence against you and will eat your flesh like fire" (James 5:1-3)

The present lesson focuses on the fourth dynasty that reigned in North Israel–the Dynasty of Jehu. This dynasty originated when God had Jehu anointed king of Israel to destroy the house of Omri for their sins. Eventually it brought the greatest material prosperity to Israel since the days of Solomon during the reign of Jeroboam II, but ironically its kings and the people under them forsook God for the worship of Baal and/or for a mere external show of religion. It was in the time of these kings that God raised up the prophets Jonah, Amos, and Hosea.

A King who went too far–Jehu (842-815 B. C.) (II Kings 9-10)

The biblical account of the reign of Jehu is taken up primarily with narratives describing the many people that he slaughtered. Jehoram, the last king of the Omri dynasty, takes the Israelite army to Ramoth-gilead to fight against Hazael of Syria. During one of the battles, Jehoram is wounded and returns to Jezreel to recover, and Ahaziah the king of Judah comes to visit him. Jehoram leaves Jehu in command of the troops at Ramoth-gilead to guard the city against Syrian attacks (8:28-29; 9:14-15). Elisha sends a prophet secretly to Ramoth-gilead to anoint Jehu king, and to instruct him to "strike down the house of Ahab" (i. e., the dynasty of Omri) to avenge the blood of the servants of the Lord that Jezebel had spilled. He announces that the dogs will lick up the blood of Jezebel in Jezreel. Jehu tells the other commanders of the army what the prophet had done and said, and charges them not to let it be known in Jezreel (9:1-16).

Jehu and his followers go to Jezreel. Jehoram and Ahaziah come out to meet them, only to discover too late that Jehu had come to kill them. As Jehoram turns to flee, Jehu shoots him in the heart with an arrow and he dies. Jehu instructs his aide, Bidkar, to cast the king's body on the plot of ground belonging to Naboth, in fulfilment of the prediction of the prophet Elijah that the "house of Ahab" (dynasty of Omri) would be cut off because Ahab had coveted Naboth's vineyard and Jezebel had had Naboth killed that her husband might have it (*I Kings* 21:21-22, 24) (*II Kings* 9:14-26).

Jehu then pursues the fleeing Ahaziah, king of Judah, and has his men shoot him. Ahaziah is able to get to Megiddo, but dies there. His servants return his body to Jerusalem, where he is buried (9:27-29).

As a part of his mission to annihilate the dynasty of Omri and to rid Israel of Baalism, Jehu returns to Jezreel to kill Jezebel. He has some eunuchs throw her out of an upper story window, and the horses trample her body. While Jehu is having a banquet in the palace, the dogs eat Jezebel's flesh, so that when Jehu's servants come to bury her, all that is left is her hands, her feet, and her skull. This fulfils Elijah's predictive announcement that the dogs would eat Jezebel in Jezreel (*I Kings* 21:23; see also *II Kings* 9:10) (*II Kings* 9:30-37).

Jehu sends letters to Samaria and tells the leaders of the city to choose one of the 70 sons of Ahab as their king to fight against him. However, the leaders are afraid of Jehu because he had killed Jehoram and Ahaziah, so they send him word that they will do whatever he says. He tells them to bring the heads of Ahab's 70 sons to him at Jezreel. They kill these men, put their heads in baskets, and take them to Jezreel. Jehu kills the rest of Ahab's house that is left at Jezreel (10:1-11).

Jehu leaves Jezreel to go to Samaria the capital to assume his role as king of Israel. On the way he meets 42 kinsmen of Ahaziah king of Judah. He has his servants kill all of them (10:12-14).

On his way to Samaria, Jehu also meets Jehonadab (Jonadab) the father of the Rechabites, who are avid worshippers of Yahweh and thus strong opponents of Baal (see *Jeremiah* 35). He has Jehonadab join him in his chariot, as he is on his way to destroy the worshippers of Baal. When he arrives in Samaria, Jehu kills the rest of Ahab's house that remains there. Then he declares deceitfully that he is going to offer a great sacrifice to Baal in the temple of Baal. He summons all the worshippers of Baal throughout Israel, and they pack the temple. Jehu offers the burnt offering, and then commands his men to kill all the worshippers of Baal. Then he burns the pillar in the temple of Baal, demolishes the temple, and makes it a latrine (10:15-28).

The Lord commends Jehu for destroying the dynasty of Omri and Baalism as he had commanded, and promises him that his dynasty will last to the fourth generation (10:30). But Jehu had gone far beyond what God had commanded in killing Ahaziah of Judah and his relatives, as is clear from the fact that Hosea declares in the time of his great-grandson Jeroboam II that the dynasty of Jehu will come to an end because of the blood that Jehu had shed at Jezreel (*Hosea* 1:4-5).

Although Jehu had put away Baalism, he continues worshipping the golden calves that Jeroboam I had erected at Dan and Bethel, and does not follow the Lord with all his heart. God punishes him by sending Hazael of Syria against Israel to capture all the territory east of Jordan for Syria (*II Kings* 10:29, 31-36). In 842 B. C., Shalmaneser III of Assyria marches against Damascus and besieges it, but is unable to take it. Then he moves on west to Phoenicia, and receives tribute from the people of Tyre and Sidon, and from Jehu. The famous Black Obelisk of Shalmaneser III shows Jehu giving tribute to the Assyrian king as an indication of his subjection to him.

Further Reduction of Israel's Power—Jehoahaz (815-801 B. C.) (II Kings 13:1-9)

Jehoahaz, the son of Jehu, replaces his father on the throne in Samaria. He persists in worshipping the golden calves at Dan and Bethel, and the Lord continues to diminish his power by sending Hazael of Syria against him. In time, Jehoahaz beseeches the Lord, and the Lord gives Israel some relief from Syria, but the military strength is greatly reduced, and Hazael captures a number of Israelite cities (see 13:25).

The Beginnings of a Revival of Military Strength—Jehoash (801-786 B. C.) (II Kings 13:10-25; 14:7-16)

Like his predecessors, Jehoash, the son of Jehoahaz, continues to worship the golden calves in Dan and Bethel. The prophet Elisha becomes very ill, and Jehoash goes to see him. Elisha tells him to shoot an arrow out the window to symbolize that Israel would be victorious against Syria. Then he tells him to strike the ground with his other arrows. Jehoash strikes the ground three times, Elisha tells him that Israel will defeat Syria in three battles, and rebukes him for not smiting the ground five or six times so that Israel might make an end of Syria (13:10-19).

Elisha dies and is buried. Once, when some Moabites make a raid in the region, the Israelites hurriedly cast the body of a dead man into Elisha's grave and flee. When his body touches Elisha's bones, he revives (13:20-21).

Hazael of Syria continues to oppress Israel. However, the Lord diminishes the power of Syria to do this successfully because he is gracious and compassionate, and faithful to his covenant with the patriarchs. According to Assyrian records and the Aramaic Inscription of Zakir, in 805 B. C., toward the end of the reign of Jehoahaz, Adad-nirari III of Assyria led an expedition into Palestine and put several nations under subjection. He greatly reduced the power of Hazael. Hazael dies in 798 B. C., and is succeeded by his son, Ben-hadad II (798-773 B. C.). These setbacks and changes in Syria gives Jehoash the opportunity he needs to resist Syria. He defeats Ben-hadad in three battles and recovers the Israelite cities that Hazael had taken from Jehoahaz (13:22-25).

Amaziah, the king of Judah, defeats the Edomites, and he

thinks this proves he is strong enough to defeat Jehoash and Israel, so he challenges Jehoash to fight him. Jehoash tries to dissuade him, but to no avail. The two armies join battle at Beth-shemesh, and Jehoash soundly defeats Amaziah. Then Jehoash comes to Jerusalem, breaks down a sizeable portion of the wall of the city, and takes as spoil to Samaria gold, silver, all the vessels of the temple and the king's treasuries, and hostages (14:7-14).

A Period of Great Prosperity—Jeroboam II (786-746 B. C.) (II Kings 14:23-29)

After the death of Adad-nirari III of Assyria (who reigned ca. 810-783 B. C), Assyria is beset with a great decline in military and economic power. Syria and Judah are also crippled because of the successes of Jehoash against Benhadad II and Amaziah respectively. This gives Jeroboam II, the son of Jehoash, opportunity to increase the power of Israel. He extends the borders of Israel from the Entrance of Hamath in the far north to the Sea of the Arabah in the far south, as was announced by the prophet Jonah, and seizes Hamath and Damascus for Israel in the process. This territorial expanse is approximately the same as that which had been controlled by Solomon (see *I Kings* 4:21, 24), and for all practical purposes it would seem that Judah is under Israelite domination during a portion of this time.

The End of the Jehu Dynasty—Zechariah (746 B. C.) (II Kings 15:8-12)

Jeroboam II is succeeded by his son Zechariah, who reigns only six months in Samaria before he is murdered by Shallum to bring the Jehu dynasty to an end. Accordingly, the dynasty of Jehu continues to the fourth generation, as the Lord had promised Jehu (see 10:30).

Three Prophets connected with Jeroboam II in North Israel— Jonah, Amos, and Hosea

The reign of Jeroboam II is very important, because it was during this time that God raised up the prophets Jonah, Amos, and Hosea.

Apparently Jonah (ca. 760 B. C.) is a man with an Israelite mentality typical of his day. His concern is the military and economic growth of his nation (*II Kings* 14:25). As the

Assyrians had caused much misery in his native land, he must have hated them greatly. Thus, when God tells him to go to Nineveh to try to bring the Assyrians to repentance so that they would not be destroyed, one can understand why he went the other way (*Jonah* 1:1-3). Even when God persuaded him to go to Nineveh, he still hated the Assyrians and did not want them to repent and be spared (*Jonah* 4).

God sends Amos from Tekoa in the territory of Judah to key cities in North Israel to condemn the Israelites for adopting customs from Baalism (*Amos* 2:7-8), increasing their wealth by oppressing the poor (2:6-7; 4:1; 5:11-12) and using dishonest business practices (8:4-6), and carrying on a religion limited to correct external acts such as offering animal sacrifices, singing, and assembling (4:4-5; 5:4-5, 21-24). He announces that Jeroboam will die by the sword, and that the Israelites will be carried away into Assyrian captivity because of their sins (7:9-17; cf. 3:11-12; 4:6-12; 5:4-5), so that the enemy will oppress them from their northernmost to their southernmost borders, i. e., "from the entrance of Hamath to the Brook of the Arabah" (6:14).

Hosea (ca. 746-724 B. C.) proclaims virtually the same message as Amos. He rebukes the people for worshipping Baal (*Hosea* 2:13; 4:11-14) and the golden calves at Dan and Bethel (8:5-6), and announces the end of the Jehu dynasty because of the blood Jehu shed at Jezreel (1:4-5), going far beyond what the Lord had instructed through his prophet (see *II Kings* 9:7-10). He announces that the Israelites will be carried into Assyrian captivity (1:4; 9:3, 6), because they trust in military strength (8:14), foreign alliances (7:8-11; 8:9; 12:1), and external acts of worship (6:4-6) rather than in God. He tries fervently to bring the people to repentance by portraying for them the compassionate and forgiving love of God as a husband who loves his wife even though she is unfaithful (1-3), or a father who loves his child even when he has denounced him and run away from home (11:1-9).

It is these prophets, and not the kings of the Jehu dynasty, who are the important spiritual giants of this troubled and corrupt period in Israelite history. (For a much more detailed discussion of these three prophets, see J. T. Willis, *My Servants the Prophets,* Vol. I).

REVIEW QUESTIONS

1. Whom did God charge to anoint Jehu king over Israel? *I Kings* 19:16. Who actually did this? *II Kings* 9:1-6. What specific command did he give Jehu? 9:7-10. Did Jehu do precisely what he commanded? *Hosea* 1:4-5. Discuss.

2. Name the different people that Jehu murdered. *II Kings* 9-10. Discuss the circumstances of the deaths of each person or group. Tell how some of these fulfilled prophetic predictions.

3. Who joined Jehu when he went to Samaria to obliterate the worshippers of Baal? *II Kings* 10:15-17. Study *Jeremiah* 35 carefully, and tell about the religion of this man's followers. How was Jehu able to kill the worshippers of Baal? *II Kings* 10:18-25.

4. Briefly list the sins of Jehu, and tell how God punished him for these sins. *II Kings* 10:29, 31-35. What do we learn about Jehu from the Black Obelisk of Shalmaneser III? Do additional research on this by reading the English translation in J. B. Pritchard, *Ancient Near Eastern texts.*

5. What sins did Jehoahaz commit? *II Kings* 13:2, 6. How did God punish him for this? 13:25. What did Elisha tell Jehoash when he came to him on his death-bed? 13:10-19. How did this come to pass historically? 13:22-25. Relate the story of Jehoash's victory over Amaziah of Judah. 14:7-14.

6. Tell the circumstances that led to the prosperity of Israel under Jeroboam II. *II Kings* 14:24-28. What prophet predicted this? 14:25. What were the extreme northern and southern boundaries of Israel at this time? 14:25; *Amos* 6:14.

7. Relate briefly the roles that the prophets Jonah, Amos, and Hosea played during the period of great prosperity under Jeroboam II. What were the major sins that Amos and Hosea condemned in North Israel? *Amos* 2:7-8; 4:1; 8:4-6; 5:21-24; *Hosea* 4:11-14; 8:5-6, 14; 7:8-11; 6:4-6. How did both of these prophets say that God was going to punish Israel for these sins? *Amos* 7:9-17; 3:11-12; 6:14; *Hosea* 1:4-5. Discuss.

Lesson VII

THE TRAUMA OF INDECISION– THE KINGDOM OF JUDAH FROM JEHOSHAPHAT TO UZZIAH (I KINGS 22:41-50; II KINGS 8:16-9:28; 11-12; 14:1-22; 15:1-7; II CHRONICLES 17-26)

"For thus said the Lord God, the Holy One of Israel,
　'In returning and rest you shall be saved;
　in quietness and in trust shall be your strength.'
And you would not, but you said,
　'No! We will speed upon horses,'
　therefore you shall speed away;
and, 'We will ride upon swift steeds,'
　therefore your pursuers shall be swift." (Isaiah 30:15-16)

During the time that the dynasties of Omri and Jehu were ruling North Israel, seven kings sat on the throne of Judah. Whereas all the kings of Israel were evil in the sight of the Lord, a few kings of Judah were, at least comparatively, considered good. Sometimes during this period, the relationships between Judah and Israel were friendly, while at other times they were hostile. Judah was faithful to the Lord part of the time, and part of the time she was not. Basically the same sins that plagued North Israel in this period also plagued Judah, such as idolatry, trusting in foreign alliances for help instead of trusting in God, attempting to increase in wealth and military strength by oppressing and neglecting the poor and oppressed, and practicing a mere external religion. As in North Israel, the greatest spirits in Judah during this time were the prophets, who fearlessly declared the word of the

Lord against all of the peoples' vices, and who exalted Yahweh and his will above every human whim and fancy.

A King who made Foreign Alliances—Jehoshaphat (873-849 B. C.) (I Kings 22:41-50; II Chronicles 17-20)

Jehoshaphat does right in the sight of the Lord, as did his father Asa. He does not worship the Baals, but sends his princes and the Levites to teach the people out of the book of the law of the Lord, and he exterminates the male cult prostitutes from the land. The Philistines and Arabs bring tribute to him, and he becomes very rich. He builds fortresses and store-cities in Judah (*I Kings* 22:41-46; *II Chronicles* 17).

In time, Jehoshaphat makes a league with wicked king Ahab of Israel, which is sealed by a political marriage between his son Jehoram and Athaliah, the daughter of Ahab and Jezebel (*II Kings* 8:18, 26-27; *II Chronicles* 18:1; 21:6; 22:2-3). Ahab urges him to go up with him to fight against Ben-hadad at Ramoth-gilead. In spite of the warning of the prophet Micaiah that if they went up Ahab would be killed, the combined armies of Israel and Judah march against Syria, are soundly defeated, and Ahab is killed (*I Kings* 22:1-40; *II Chronicles* 18; this battle and the role of Micaiah in this incident are discussed at length in Lesson IV under Ahab). When Jehoshaphat returns to Jerusalem from the battle of Ramoth-gilead, the prophet Jehu meets him and condemns him for making an alliance with such a wicked man as Ahab (*II Chronicles* 19:1-3). Jehoshaphat appoints judges and Levites to hear and decide on legal cases in the land. He gives them this charge, which would be an ideal standard for any judge: "Now then, let the fear of the Lord be upon you; take heed what you do, for there is no perversion of justice with the Lord our God, or partiality, or taking bribes" (19:7). Undoubtedly these corrupt practices were rather widespread in Judah (as they were in Israel), because they are condemned a short time later by Isaiah and Micah (see *Isaiah* 1:16-17, 23; 10:1-4; *Micah* 3:9-11), and apparently Jehoshaphat is attempting to stem the tide of corruption here (*II Chronicles* 19:4-11).

The Moabites, Ammonites, and Edomites march toward Jerusalem to fight against Jehoshaphat. He proclaims a fast, and prays to the Lord to intervene and deliver Judah. This prayer is a model of deep trust in God. Jehoshaphat begins by acknowledging that the Lord is ruler over all the kingdoms of the earth (20:6). (It is not true, then, that in Old Testament times the Jews believed that God was a national God, limited in his activity to the land of Canaan!). He praises God for having given the land of Canaan to his people, and states that when Solomon built the temple he prayed that when affliction came on Israel, if the people would pray toward this house God would hear and deliver them (20:7-9; cf. *I Kings* 8:37-40, 44-45, *II Chronicles* 6:28-31, 34-35). Jehoshaphat realistically admits, "We are powerless against this great multitude . . . We do not know what to do, but our eyes are upon thee" (20:12). It is this kind of attitude in prayer that God desires and accepts. Thus, the Spirit of the Lord comes on a certain Levite named Jahaziel, and he encourages the people not to fear, because the battle is not theirs but God's. He declares that they will not even have to fight, but the Lord will give them the victory. Then Jehoshaphat and the people worship and praise God (20:1-19).

The next morning, when the enemy armies plan to attack, Jehoshaphat urges the people, "Believe in the Lord your God, and you will be established; believe his prophets, and you will succeed" (20:20). The Lord sets an ambush against the attackers, and the Ammonites and Moabites turn on the Edomites and destroy them, and then they begin fighting and killing each other. The Judeans call the valley where this battle takes place Beracah, which is the Hebrew word for "Blessing," because there they "blessed" the Lord for giving them the victory. They return to Jerusalem with much spoil and rejoicing. It is significant that this victory had a major impact on all the kingdoms round about (20:29), for God had chosen Israel as his means of trying to reach the nations by word (see the book of *Jonah; Isaiah* 43:8-12) and example. When the nations saw clear evidence of God working in behalf of his chosen people, they could perceive his power and love, and thereby had good reason to forsake their powerless false gods and to turn in penitence and obedience to the true God of the universe (see *Genesis* 12:1-3; *Joshua* 4:23-24; *I Samuel* 17:46).

44

On another occasion, Jehoshaphat makes an entangling alliance with the wicked King Ahaziah of Israel, to build ships at Ezion-geber to go to Tarshish. But the prophet Eliezer rebukes him for making this league, and announces that the ships will be wrecked (*II Chronicles* 20:35-37). When Ahaziah proposes that they attempt this a second time, Jehoshaphat refuses (*I Kings* 22:48-49).

By way of summary, it should be mentioned that three prophets are connected with Jehoshaphat: (1) Micaiah, who warned him and Ahab not to go against the Syrians at Ramoth-gilead; (2) Jehu, who rebuked him for making an alliance with Ahab; and (3) Eliezer, who condemned him for making a league with Ahaziah. All these prophets staunchly oppose the practice of God's people making alliances with wicked kings and nations; instead, they should put their trust in the Lord. In principle, the Christian is faced with the same alternative: in critical situations, he can either trust in God completely for help, or he can go to wicked men, who often appear to have the solution to life's problems when actually they do not. As Peter puts it, such people "promise . . . freedom, but they themselves are slaves to corruption" (*II Peter* 2:19).

Another King influenced by a Wicked Wife—Jehoram (849-842 B. C.) (II Kings 8:16-24; II Chronicles 21)
The Bible relates numerous instances of the adverse affects of the influence of a wicked wife on a man. Solomon married foreign women and they turned away his heart after other gods (*I Kings* 11:1-8). Ahab married Jezebel, a Phoenician princess who was a zealous worshipper of Baal, and promoted the worship of this foreign god throughout the land of Israel (16:31-33). And now, in order to seal a political alliance with Ahab of Israel, Jehoshaphat had given his son Jehoram in marriage to Athaliah, the daughter of Ahab and Jezebel. Under his influence, Jehoram follows the practices of the kings of the Omri dynasty in North Israel (*II Kings* 8:18; *II Chronicles* 21:6). He murders his brothers and some of the princes of Judah, apparently because they oppose his ascension to the throne because he does not follow the Lord (*II Chronicles* 21:2-4). He builds high places in the hill country of Judah, and encourages the people to go astray from God (21:11).

The Lord punishes Jehoram in two ways because of his apostasy: (1) he raises up against him a number of nations to fight against him: the Edomites, Libnah, the Philistines, and the Arabs (21:8-10, 16-17); (2) he has a letter sent to him from Elijah, announcing that a great plague would fall on the people and that Jehoram would die of an incurable bowel disease, all of which comes to pass (21:12-19).

A King who followed His Mother's Wicked Counsel—Ahaziah (842 B. C.) (II Kings 8:25-29; II Chronicles 22:1-9)

Jehoram is succeeded by his son Ahaziah, who is also the son of Athaliah, the wicked daughter of Ahab and Jezebel. Ahaziah follows the counsel of his mother, and thus (like his father Jehoram) adopts the wicked practices of the North Israelite dynasty of Omri. At the advice of his mother and other counselors, Ahaziah allies with Jehoram of Israel (the brother of Athaliah!) to fight against Hazael at Ramoth-gilead. Jehoram is wounded during a battle and retires to Jezreel, where Ahaziah comes to visit him. While they are there, Elisha has a prophet anoint Jehu king of Israel. Jehu's first action is to go to Jezreel and murder Jehoram of Israel and Ahaziah of Judah. Thus God punished Ahaziah for his wickedness. (A much fuller account of these events is given in Lesson III under Jehoram of Israel.)

Judah is Ruled by a Wicked Woman—Athaliah (842-837 B. C.) (II Kings 11:1-20; II Chronicles 22:10-23:21)

It is ironical that because of her marriage to Jehoram of Judah, and due to the deaths of Jehoram and her son Ahaziah, Athaliah, the daughter of Ahab and Jezebel, and thus a North Israelite (!) princess, becomes queen of Judah (!) by quickly taking matters into her own hands. To rid herself of any rivals, Athaliah kills all the royal family of Judah, except that Jehosheba the daughter of Jehoram of Judah steals away the year-old youngest son of Ahaziah named Joash, and hides him in the temple. She plunders the temple and uses all its dedicated things for the Baals (*II Chronicles* 24:7). After Athaliah has reigned six years, Jehosheba's husband, Jehoiada the priest, makes a covenant with certain captains in Judah to set up Joash as king. When Athaliah learns what has happened, there is nothing she can do. Jehoiada has her slain, and then makes a covenant with the people that they should worship the Lord. They tear down the temple of Baal, break in pieces his altars and images, and kill Mattan the priest of Baal. Then they install Joash as king.

Restoration and Renewed Apostasy—Joash (837-800 B. C.)
(II Kings 11:21-12:21; II Chronicles 24)
The actions of Joash pose a real enigma, which once again underlines the power of sin in the world. Here is a man who received good training in his youth by a godly priest, Jehoiada, who invested a great deal of energy and money in repairing the temple which his predecessor and wicked rival, Athaliah, had plundered for Baal, but who later goes into idolatry himself and kills the righteous son of the godly man who saved his life and trained him in the right ways of the Lord. His apostasy was due to the fact that he listened to the princes of Judah after the death of Jehoiada (*II Chronicles* 24:17), which powerfully illustrates the truth of the statement, "Do not be deceived: 'Bad company ruins good morals' " (*I Corinthians* 15:33).

Apparently ca. 815 B. C. or so, Joash instructs the priests and Levites to gather money from the people to pay workers to repair the temple which Athaliah had plundered and desecrated, but the Levites are not enthusiastic about this and so move very slowly. When Joash confronts Joiada about this, the priests go so far as to decide not to repair the temple. But at the command of Joash, Jehoiada sets up a chest beside the altar with a hole bored in it, and the people cast in money as they pass by. With this, the workmen, carpenters, builders, masons, and stonecutters are paid to repair the temple, and the rest of the money is used to make utensils to carry on the temple worship.

Jehoiada dies at the age of 130. After this, Joash hearkens to the advice of the princes of Judah, forsakes the temple worship, and serves the Asherim and the idols. God sends prophets to bring Joash and the Judeans to repentance, but to no avail. Then the Spirit of God comes on Jehoiada's son Zechariah, and he rebukes the people for forsaking the Lord. Joash commands that he be stoned to death (see *Matthew* 23:35; *Luke* 11:51), thereby manifesting total ingratitude for all that Jehoiada had done for him in his early years. As punishment for this, the Lord raises up the Syrians under

Hazael. They take Gath in the land of the Philistines, but Joash sends Hazael all the votive gifts that his predecessors (Jehoshaphat, Jehoram, and Ahaziah) had dedicated, his own votive gifts, and the gold in the temple and the king's palace to get him to leave Jerusalem. At a later time, apparently, Hazael attacks Judah, destroys the princes that had advised Joash to forsake the Lord, takes the spoil of Judah to Damascus, and leaves Joash badly wounded. Two of Joash's servants take advantage of the situation and murder him to avenge the blood of Zechariah.

A Fickle King whom God Punished—Amaziah (800-783 B. C.) (II Kings 14:1-20; II Chronicles 25)

Joash's son Amaziah receives the throne of Judah, and kills the two men that murdered his father. He makes a league with North Israel to fight against the Edomites, but a prophet tells him to break the pact because the Lord is not with Israel, and the Lord does not need great numbers of men to win a battle. Amaziah defeats the Edomites without Israel, but he brings the gods of Edom, worships them, and offers offerings to them.

A prophet rebukes Amaziah for worshipping false gods, and tells him he will be destroyed for this. Amaziah thinks that because he defeated the Edomites he can also defeat Israel. So he challenges Jehoash of Israel to a battle at Beth-shemesh. Jehoash tries to dissuade him, but Amaziah stubbornly insists. Israel wins a mighty victory over Judah, Jehoash captures Amaziah, brings him to Jerusalem, and breaks down a large portion of the wall. He takes as spoil gold and silver, the treasures in the temple and the king's palace, and hostages. (For further details, see Lesson IV).

When Amaziah turns away from the Lord to worship the gods of Edom, they make a conspiracy against him in Jerusalem. He flees to Lachish, but they pursue him and kill him there.

A King who became a Leper—Uzziah (783-742 B. C.) (II Kings 15:1-7; II Chronicles 26)

The people of Judah make Uzziah (Azariah) king in place of his father. Because of the great military and economic strength of Jeroboam II in Israel (who possibly had a great deal of power in Judah as well), and because of the weakened condition of Assyria, Uzziah is able to build up the military and economic strength of Judah. He builds Elath near the Gulf of Aqabah and restores it to Judah. He defeats the Philistines, the Arabs, and the Edomites, and the Ammonites pay tribute to him. He promotes agricultural pursuits, which become very prosperous in Judah. He builds a powerful army with the most modern weapons. Among other things, he makes engines to be on the towers and corners of the Jerusalem wall to shoot arrows and large stones against attacking armies.

However, all of this success makes Uzziah proud and arrogant. He goes to the temple to burn incense himself on the altar of incense. The priest Azariah tries to stop him, because God had designated the priests alone to offer such sacrifices, but to no avail. Uzziah becomes angry at the priest, and the Lord smites him with leprosy. The priests rush Uzziah out of the temple, he is banned from entering the temple again, and is forced to live in a separate house. During the last several years of his life, his son Jotham rules the people as regent. It is significant that Isaiah received his call to be a prophet in the year that king Uzziah died (742 B. C.; cf. *Isaiah* 6:1), although the Bible does not make it clear whether Uzziah was still alive at the time. *II Chronicles* 26.23 states that they buried Jotham in the burial field which belonged to the kings. In light of this, it is interesting that in 1931 archeologists uncovered a carved stone tablet on the Mount of Olives dating from the first century B. C. and inscribed in Aramaic, which reads: "Hither were brought the bones of Uzziah, king of Judah—do not open!"

REVIEW QUESTIONS

1. Relate some of Jehoshaphat's successful undertakings. *I Kings* 22:41-46; *II Chronicles* 17. Tell of his alliance with Ahab. How did he seal this alliance? *II Kings* 8:18, 26-27; *II Chronicles* 18:1; 21:6; 22:2-3. Who was the prophet that warned them not to go up against Ben-hadad at Ramoth-gilead? What happened to Ahab in this battle? *I Kings* 22:1-40. Who was the prophet that rebuked Jehoshaphat for making a league with Ahab? *II Chronicles* 19:1-3.

2. What instructions did Jehoshaphat give the judges and Levites that he appointed to hear court cases in Judah? *II Chronicles* 19:7. What practical lessons can modern judges learn from these? Discuss.

3. Tell how Jehoshaphat manifested his faith in God when the Judeans were attacked by the Moabites, Ammonites, and Edomites. *II Chronicles* 20:1-19. Discuss practical applications that such faith has for Christians today. What effect did Judah's victory have on the surrounding nations? 20:29. What does this indicate about God's intention in choosing Israel? Answer this in light of *Genesis* 12:1-3; *Joshua* 4:23-24; *I Samuel* 17:46; and similar passages. Discuss at length.

4. Who had a great influence on Jehoram king of Judah? Was this influence good or bad? *II Kings* 8:18; *II Chronicles* 21:6. In what two ways did God punish Jehoram for forsaking him for the Baals? *II Chronicles* 21:12-19.

5. Who was Ahaziah's counselor? *II Chronicles* 22:3. With whom did he make an entangling alliance? For what purpose was this alliance made? What happened to Ahaziah's ally? What did Ahaziah do? Relate the story of Ahaziah's death. 22:5-9; *II Kings* 8:28-9:29.

6. Tell how Athaliah got the throne of Judah and how she lost it. *II Kings* 11:1-20; *II Chronicles* 22:10-23:21. Who was the priest that saved Joash's life and trained him to serve the Lord? *II Kings* 11:2. What great work did Joash do about midway through his reign? 12:4-16. After Jehoiada's death, what great sins did Joash commit? *II Chronicles* 24:17-22. How did God punish him for this? 24:23-24. How did Joash die? 24:25-26.

7. What foolish thing did Amaziah do after he defeated the Edomites? *II Chronicles* 25:14. How did God punish him for this? 25:17-28. Discuss verse 20.

8. Relate the successful undertakings of Uzziah. *II Chronicles* 26:2, 5:15. How did he react to his successes? 26:16. What sin did he commit in the temple? 26:16-19. How did God punish him for this? 26:19-21. Who governed the people as regent the rest of his life? 26:21. What prophet received his call in the year Uzziah died? *Isaiah* 6:1.

Lesson VIII

THE CERTAINTY OF GOD'S DAY OF RECKONING– THE ASSYRIAN CAPTIVITY OF NORTH ISRAEL (II KINGS 15:13-20:21; II CHRONICLES 27-32; ISAIAH 36-39)

"Woe to those who put far away the evil day,
and bring near the seat of violence" (Amos 6:3)

.The longer Israel continued to exist, the more sinful she became. All of her kings and many of her people followed the lead of Jeroboam I in worshipping the golden calves at Dan and Bethel, in adopting the fertility rites of Canaanite and Phoenician Baalism, in practicing a mere external form of religion, and in oppressing the poor in order to increase their own wealth and power. Such rampant and incessant sinning could only bring destruction in due time. Sin is like a seed. It produces punishment in the life of the sinner. The sinner actually destroys himself (see *Proverbs* 13:13, 21; *Isaiah* 3:9; *Jeremiah* 2:17). It is little wonder, then, that God declared to North Israel: "The end has come upon my people Israel" (*Amos* 8:2). This lesson deals with the last days of the Northern kingdom, and with major events in Judah in this period and shortly thereafter. The instability and corruption that existed in North Israel in this time are vividly illustrated by the series of rapid-fire murders of her kings. Only the brief reigns of Menahem and his son Pekahiah can be regarded as a final (fifth) attempt at establishing a dynasty in Israel, and it was very weak and soon failed.

The Last Days of North Israel (II Kings 15:13-31, 37; 16:1-9; 17:1-6; II Chronicles 28:1-21)
   The vicissitudes of Israel and Judah are so inseparably

intertwined during the last 25 years of Israel's existence that it will be necessary to discuss both kingdoms at the same time to some extent, especially in the interaction between Pekah of Israel and Ahaz of Judah. The events in the history of North Israel are the guiding lines in this section of study.

1. *Shallum* (746 B. C.) (*II Kings* 15:13-16). Shallum gains the throne of Israel by murdering Zechariah, the last member of the Jehu dynasty. After a reign of only one month, Menahem sacks Tappuah (often identified with Beit Nettif located ca. 12 miles west of Bethlehem, although this is not certain) and murders Shallum at Samaria.

2. *Menahem* (745-738 B. C.) (*II Kings* 15:17-22). Because Menahem persists in the sins of Jeroboam I, God raises up against Israel the Assyrians under Tiglath-pileser III (745-727 B. C.) or Pul. In 743-742 and again in 738, Tiglath-pileser invades the Western States, and according to his Assyrian annals takes heavy tribute from Rezon (Rezin) of Syria, Menahem of Israel, and other kings. One reason that Menahem pays him tribute is "that he might help him to confirm his hold of the royal power" (15:19). By piecing bits of information together, it seems likely that Pekah was ruling the region of Galilee (in northern Israel) and Gilead (east of the Jordan) as an anti-Assyrian during the reigns of Menahem and Pekahiah (see 15:25, 29; 16:5), and that his twenty year reign (15:27) includes that time. Menahem, taking a pro-Assyrian political stance, is able to survive because Tiglath-pileser protects him against Pekah in return for a large annual tribute. It is ironic that Menahem is forced to tax the wealthy leading citizens of Israel, who had oppressed the poor so greatly to secure their riches, in order to pay Assyria (15:20). This recalls the warnings of Amos that the rich would not be able to enjoy their possessions (*Amos* 3:13-15; 5:11-12; 6:11-14).

3. *Pekahiah* (738-738 B. C.) (*II Kings* 15:23-26). Pekahiah undoubtedly continues the policy of his father Menahem to send annual tribute to Tiglath-pileser of Assyria, and thus is to be regarded as pro- Assyrian politically. Pekah, his captain who rises up and kills him for the throne in Samaria, is apparently anti-Assyrian, which explains his rebellion against that power.

4. *Pekah* (737-732 B. C.) (*II Kings* 15:27-31, 37; 16:1-9; *II Chronicles* 28:1-21). Pekah's twenty year reign (*II Kings* 15:27) apparently includes several years in which he was ruling over Galilee and Gilead simultaneous with the reigns of Menahem and Pekahiah over Samaria. In ca. 735 B. C., he and Rezin of Syria instigate a rebellion against Assyria among the Western States. However, Jotham (15:37), and after him his son Ahaz of Judah, refuse to join with them. Consequently, they bring their armies to Jerusalem with the intention of dethroning Ahaz and setting the son of Tabeel, an anti-Assyrian, on the throne (*Isaiah* 7:1-6). The Edomites and Philistines take advantage of the situation to invade Judah from the south and west to take captives and spoil. The Israelites and Syrians humble Ahaz and take several thousand captives to Damascus and Samaria, but at the word of the prophet Oded the Israelites release them (*II Chronicles* 28:5-15). Ahaz sends to Tiglath-pileser for help against the invaders, the Assyrians attack Syria and Israel in ca. 732 B. C., and take the inhabitants of Damascus (*II Kings* 16:9) and the people of Galilee and Gilead (the territory which Pekah had originally controlled) into exile (15:29). This may be termed the First Stage of the Assyrian Captivity of North Israel. Hoshea conspires against Pekah and kills him to gain the throne (15:30). Apparently these losses and defeats are divine punishments for North Israel's continued apostasy.

5. *Hosea* (732-724 B. C.) (*II Kings* 17:1-6). Tiglath-pileser claims in his annals that he put Hoshea on the throne of Israel, and this is undoubtedly correct in the sense that no one could have taken the throne of Israel at this juncture in history without Assyrian approval, in light of Pekah's rebellion against that power. Probably when Tiglath-pileser dies in 727 and his son Shalmaneser V (727-722 B. C.) takes the throne of Assyria, Hoshea decides to rebel with the support of Egypt under So (Sewe). In retaliation, Shalmaneser brings the Assyrian army against Samaria and besieges the city for three years (724-721 B. C.). Toward the end of the siege, Shalmaneser dies and is succeeded by Sargon II (722-705 B. C.). In his annals Sargon claims to have taken the city and carried a large number of its inhabitants into exile, and this is undoubtedly the case. Samaria falls in 721 B. C. This may be termed the Second Stage of the Assyrian Captivity of North Israel.

The Reasons for Israel's Fall (II Kings 17:7-41)

The inspired author of I-II Kings is more concerned with why Israel fell than with the details of that fall. He cites the following reasons: (1) they had sinned against the Lord who had brought them out of Egypt (verse 7); (2) they had worshipped other gods (verses 7, 15); (3) they had adopted the customs of the nations and the customs which Jeroboam I had introduced when he became ruler of the ten northern tribes (verses 8, 15, 16, 21-22; see *I Kings* 12:28-33); (4) they had built high places and adopted Canaanite Baalism (verses 9-12, 16); (5) they had not listened to the prophets whom the Lord had sent to bring them to repentance (verses 13-15); (6) they had burned their sons and daughters as sacrifices and had practiced divination and sorcery (verse 17).

In place of the Israelites that had been carried into Assyrian captivity, Sargon brings peoples from the Mesopotamian region to inhabit Samaria in place of the Israelites. They do not worship the Lord, so he sends lions among them to devour them. Sargon sends an Israelite priest to Bethel to teach them Yahweh was to be worshipped. They worship their own gods and Yahweh (verses 24-41). The Israelites left in the northern territory intermarry with the foreigners who settle there, producing a hybrid race called the Samaritans.

The History of Judah at the Time of Israel's Fall (II Kings 15:32-16:20; II Chronicles 27-32; Isaiah 36-39)

During the last years of Israel's existence, three kings reigned over Judah. This was the era in which two of the great prophets of Judah did their work: Isaiah and Micah. (For a detailed study of these two prophets, see J. T. Willis, *My Servants the Prophets,* Vol. II).

1. *Jotham* (750 [742]-735 B. C.) (*II Kings* 15:32-38; *II Chronicles* 27). Jotham's reign of 16 years apparently includes ca. 8 years when he was regent under his father Uzziah after he had been banished to a separate house when he was smitten with leprosy (*II Kings* 15:5; *II Chronicles* 26:21). Jotham continues the building programs of Uzziah. He builds the upper gate of the temple, much of the wall of Ophel, cities in the hill country of Judah, and forts and towers on the wooded hills. He defeats the Ammonites, and they are forced to pay him annual tribute for three years.

Toward the end of his reign, Rezin of Syria and Pekah of Israel begin invasions into Judah when they learn that Jotham will not join them in a rebellion against Assyria. It is interesting that archeologists have discovered a seal at Ezion-geber with the inscription "belonging to Jotham." Scholars generally agree that this must be king Jotham of Judah, the son of Uzziah.

2. *Ahaz* (735-715 B. C.) (*II Kings* 16; *II Chronicles* 28). Ahaz is a wicked king who carries Judah into deep corruption. He makes molten images for the Baals, burns his sons as an offering, and sacrifices on the high places. As a punishment for this, the Lord raises up Pekah of Israel and Rezin of Syria against Judah because Ahaz refuses to join their rebellion against Tiglath-pileser of Assyria. They march on Jerusalem with the intention of dethroning Ahaz and putting on the throne the son of Tabeel, an anti-Assyrian politically (*Isaiah* 7:1-6). They kill many Judeans and carry off large numbers of the population to Damascus and Samaria. The Edomites and Philistines take advantage of the situation to invade Judah from the south and west, and also carry off spoils and captives. The prophet Oded rebukes the Israelites for carrying off their kinsmen, and tells them to return them to Judah. Ahaz is extremely fearful of Pekah and Rezin, and, against the counsel of Isaiah (*Isaiah* 7:3-17; 8:1-10), sends to Tiglath-pileser for help. The Assyrians march against Syria and Israel ca. 732 B. C., and carry off the people of Damascus (*II Kings* 16:9) and of Galilee and Gilead (15:29) into captivity (*II Kings* 16:1-9; *II Chronicles* 28:1-21).

However, Ahaz's entangling alliance with Tiglath-pileser extends beyond the defeat of their common enemies, to Judah's detriment. The common belief in the ancient Near East was that when a large, well-fortified city like Damascus fell, it was because the god of that city was angry with its inhabitants and gave them into the hands of their enemies. Therefore, the victors honored and worshipped the god of the defeated city for giving them the victory. In order to impress Tiglath-pileser, then, Ahaz goes to Damascus to meet him, has his priest in Jerusalem named Uriah build an altar there like the one in Damascus, worships the gods of Damascus because Rezin had overrun him earlier, and sets up this altar before the temple to replace the altar that

Solomon built. In order to further please Tiglath-pileser, and perhaps also to secure enough precious metal to be able to pay him annual tribute, Ahaz cuts off the frames of the laver stands, removes the lavers from them, takes down the molten sea from the bronze oxen supporting them, and removes the covered way for the sabbath inside the palace and the outer entrance for the king from the house of the Lord. He shuts the doors of the temple, erects heathen altars in Jerusalem, and makes high places to burn incense to other gods in every city in Judah (*II Kings* 16:10-20; *II Chronicles* 28:22-27).

3. *Hezekiah* (715-687 B. C.) (*II Kings* 18-20; *II Chronicles* 29-32; *Isaiah* 36-39). There are a number of critical problems pertaining to the reign of Hezekiah which cannot be treated in a booklet of this nature. One is the problem of the date of the beginning of Hezekiah's reign (*II Kings* 18:9 would seem to suggest 727, while 18:13 would seem to suggest 715). Another is the role of Tirhakah in the Egyptian regime when Sennacherib invaded Jerusalem in 701 B. C. (see 19:9). Still another is the question of whether Sennacherib invaded Jerusalem once or twice. The student who is interested in pursuing these questions in depth should consult good commentaries, journal articles, and articles in Biblical encyclopedias and dictionaries on these issues.

The biblical account of Hezekiah's reign does not seem to be in exact chronological order, but the major emphasis of this presentation is clear: the inspired writers emphasize the struggles that Hezekiah had with his faith as various crises flooded into his life and into the life of Judah. The reign of Hezekiah seems to center around three major events.

(a) Not long after Hezekiah takes the throne, he inaugurates a far-reaching religious and political reform in Judah, which was badly needed after the corruption that Ahaz had introduced and perpetrated in the land. He removes the high places, breaks the pillars, cuts down the Asherah, demolishes the bronze serpent that Moses had made in the wilderness for the people to view when they were bitten by snakes (see *Numbers* 21:9), which the people had called Nehushtan and had made an object of worship, and keeps the commandments which the Lord had commanded Moses. He drives out the Philistines, who had invaded Judah in the days of Ahaz because Judah had been greatly weakened by the forces of Rezin and Pekah as a punishment for Ahaz's sins (*II Chronicles* 28:18-19). (*II Kings* 18:1-8). He opens the doors of the temple which Ahaz had shut (see *II Chronicles* 28:24) and repairs them, sets Levites and Aaronic priests over the temple worship, cleanses the temple, offers a mighty sin offering to make atonement for all Israel, and reinstates the authorized singers and musicians in the temple (*II Chronicles* 29). He invites all the North Israelites who are left after the Assyrian Captivity and all the Judeans to come to Jerusalem on the fourteenth day of the second month to keep the Passover. Many come, and the people are so overjoyed by the reform that they keep the Passover fourteen days rather than the normal seven (*II Chronicles* 30). Hezekiah commands that all the offerings commanded in the Law of Moses be revived by the Levites and priests, he has tithes paid to the priests and Levites to sustain them, and he repairs the rooms around the .temple for their dwellings (*II Chronicles* 31). He makes treasuries for all precious metals, storehouses for produce, and stalls for livestock. He has a tunnel dug through solid rock under a portion of Jerusalem as a conduit to bring water from the Gihon Spring into the city (*II Kings* 20:20; *II Chronicles* 32:27-30). Archeologists have discovered an inscription in this Siloam tunnel describing the work of Hezekiah's servants on the conduit.

(b) In 705 B. C., Sargon II died and was succeeded by Sennacherib on the Assyrian throne. As was common when a new king came on the throne, several of the nations subject to Assyria rebelled. Merodach-baladan II of Babylon rebels in the east, and Shabako the Ethiopian ruler of Egypt and Hezekiah of Judah rebel in the west. About 702 B. C. (since Hezekiah's life was lengthened 15 years, *II Kings* 20:6, and since apparently he died in 687 B. C.), Hezekiah becomes very sick with a boil, and Isaiah tells him he will die. However, the king prays fervently to the Lord, and the Lord heals him and lengthens his life 15 years. Isaiah has a cake of figs placed on the boil, and Hezekiah recovers. The Lord causes the shadow on the sundial of Ahaz to turn back ten steps as a sign to Hezekiah that he will heal him and that he will deliver Jerusalem from the Assyrians (*II Kings* 20:1-11; *II Chronicles* 32:24; *Isaiah* 38:1-8, 21-22). Hezekiah composes a beautiful poem, praising the Lord for delivering him (*Isaiah* 38:9-20).

(c) Apparently in order to persuade Hezekiah to join him in a rebellion against Sennacherib, when Merodach-baladan II of Babylon learns that Hezekiah had been sick and had recovered, he sends a good will embassy to him. Hezekiah receives the messengers gladly and shows them all his treasures, evidently meaning that he agreed to the proposed alliance. Isaiah rebukes Hezekiah for making this foreign alliance, and announces that eventually Judah will be carried into Babylonian captivity (*II Kings* 20:12-21; *II Chronicles* 32:31; *Isaiah* 39).

Sennacherib immediately reacts. He puts down Merodach-baladan's uprising in the east, then moves west in 701 B. C. He attacks and conquers Lachish about 25 miles southwest of Jerusalem, sets up headquarters there, and sends one section of his army under his officer, the Rabshakeh, to besiege Jerusalem. Hezekiah is very fearful at first, and sends Sennacherib large amounts of silver and gold as tribute to try to persuade him to withdraw the siege (*II Kings* 18:13-16). Against the earnest pleas of Isaiah (see *Isaiah* 30:1-7; 31:1-3), Hezekiah sends to Egypt for help, but she has little power against the Assyrians. While the Assyrians are around Jerusalem, the Rabshakeh tries to break down the morale of the Jews on the wall defending the city by chiding them for *trusting* in Egypt, the Lord, and Hezekiah. The words he uses for "trust" are very descriptive of the true nature of this vital element of godly living: "rest" (*II Kings* 18:19), "confidence" (verse 19), "leaning" (verse 21), and "relying" (verses 21, 22, 30). Hezekiah charges the people not to be afraid of the Assyrians, but to "be strong and of good courage . . .; there is one greater with us that with him. With him is an arm of flesh; but with us is the Lord our God, to help us and to fight our battles" (*II Chronicles* 32:7-8).

When the Egyptians attack the Assyrians from the south at Libnah, Sennacherib sends a letter to Hezekiah demanding that he surrender. Hezekiah goes to the temple, spreads out the letter before the Lord, and prays that he will overthrow the Assyrians "that all the kingdoms of the earth may know that thou, O Lord, art God alone" (*II Kings* 19:19). It will be noted that here again the Jews recognize that God chose them to be his instrument to try to bring the world to repentance and conversion by teaching and example (see *Genesis* 12:1-3; *Joshua* 4:23-24; *I Samuel* 17:46; *I Kings* 8:60; *II Kings* 5:15). When the nations see God working in the lives of the Israelites, they are able to understand his power and wisdom and love—his true nature—and they will be constrained to turn from their false gods to him. In answer to Hezekiah's prayer, that night an angel of God passes through the Assyrian camp and slays 185,000 soldiers. Sennacherib returns to Nineveh and eventually is killed by his sons (*II Kings* 19:8-37; *Isaiah* 37:5-38).

Hezekiah was able to pray to the Lord to spare his life when he had the boil, and to deliver Jerusalem from Sennacherib and the Assyrians, because he believed that God alone is "the living God" (*II Kings* 19:4, 16), who made heaven and earth, and who is king over all the kingdoms of the earth (19:15). It is incongruous for a person to pray to God unless he believes that God really exists, that he is alive, and that he can and will do things for man that are impossible for man to do for himself by his own strength and wisdom (see *Ephesians* 3:20-21; *Philippians* 4:5-7).

REVIEW QUESTIONS

1. Who was Menahem's opponent in Israel throughout his reign? *II Kings* 15:19, 25. Who helped Menahem stay in control of Israel as long as he did? 15:19. What did Menahem have to do to gain and keep this help? 15:20. Where did he get his money for this? Discuss the irony of this situation, and make applications to modern needs and situations.

2. Who were the kings of Syria and Israel that led a rebellion against Tiglath-pileser III of Assyria? *II Kings* 16:5. Why did they besiege Jerusalem? *II Chronicles* 28:1-6; *Isaiah* 7:5-6. What other nations also besieged Jerusalem at this time? *II Chronicles* 28:16-19. How did Isaiah advise Ahaz to deal with this crisis? *Isaiah* 7:7-9. How did Ahaz deal with it? *II Kings* 16:7-8. What territories did Tiglath-pileser overrun in 732 B. C.? *II Kings* 16:9; 15:29.

3. Who was the last king of Israel? *II Kings* 17:1. Who was the king of Assyria against whom he rebelled? 17:3-4. Whom did he take as an ally? 17:4. Who was the king of Assyria that actually captured Samaria? According to the Bible, for what six sins did God have Assyria carry his people of Israel into captivity? 17:7-17. Do any of these sins exist in the church and/or world today? Discuss the relationship between sin and punishment suggested in this text.

4. Enumerate the sins of Ahaz of Judah. *II Kings* 16:3-4; *II Chronicles* 23:2-4. How did God punish him and Judah for these? *II Chronicles* 28:5-8. What role did the prophet Oded play in this situation? 28:9-11.

5. Tell how Ahaz's entangling alliance with Tiglath-pileser III got Judah into deep spiritual trouble. *II Kings* 16:10-20. What ungodly things did Ahaz do to try to please the Assyrian king? What lessons can modern Christians learn from this?

6. State the three major events that the Bible records in the reign of Hezekiah. *II Kings* 18-20; *II Chronicles* 29-32. Discuss each event, and make modern applications.

7. Who was the Babylonian king that sent messengers to Hezekiah to tell him how glad he was that he had recovered from his boil? *II Kings* 20:12. How did Hezekiah treat these messengers? 20:13. What did Isaiah think about this? What did he predict in relationship to it? 20:16-18.

8. Briefly describe the two incidents in which Hezekiah prayed to God. *II Kings* 20:2; 19:15. What are some of the basic presuppositions of prayer? 19:4, 16. Explain verse 19, and discuss its significance.

9. The Rabshakeh chided the Jews on the wall of Jerusalem for trusting in what three things? *II Kings* 18:21, 22, 29, 30. What four words does he use for "trust"? 18:19, 22, 29-30. Discuss the concept of "trust" or "faith" in the Bible in light of this.

Lesson IX

AN ANCIENT RESTORATION MOVEMENT – THE WORK OF JOSIAH
II KINGS 21:1-23:30; II CHRONICLES 33-35)

"Thus says the Lord:
'Stand by the roads, and look,
and ask for the ancient paths,
where the good way is; and walk in it,
and find rest for your souls' " (Jeremiah 6:16)

Hezekiah's attempt to bring Judah back to a deep commitment to and trust in God was short-lived. After his death, Judah was plunged into deep sin and corruption under Manasseh and Amon. Afterwards, Josiah made a valiant effort to restore God's people to their first love, but was only partially successful, so that it was not too long until Judah was carried into Babylonian captivity. The present lesson deals with the reigns of Manasseh, Amon, and Josiah.

A King who Failed his People—Manasseh (687-642 B. C.) (II Kings 21:1-18; II Chronicles 33:1-20)
During his long reign, Manasseh reverses the reform measures of Hezekiah and reverts back to the evil ways of Ahaz. He rebuilds the high places Hezekiah had destroyed, erects altars for the Baals, makes Asherahs, and worships the sun, moon, and stars like the nations around Judah. Like Ahaz (see *II Kings* 16:3), he burns his sons as a sacrifice, and practices various kinds of witchcraft. He also sheds much innocent blood in Jerusalem. Because of these sins, God sends his servants the prophets to announce that just as he had carried Israel into exile, he would soon take Judah into exile (*II Kings* 21:1-18; *II Chronicles* 33:1-9).

61

To punish Manasseh for his sins, the Lord raises up the Assyrians against him. They besiege Jerusalem, capture him, and take him into exile to Babylon. Assyrian inscriptions refer to a rebellion against Assyria by Babylon and some Western States ca. 652-648 B. C. Manasseh probably participated in this rebellion. When it was put down in 648, the Assyrian king Ashurbanipal (669-630 B. C.) spent a great deal of time in Babylon, probably to make sure the Babylonians did not rebel against Assyria again. This may be why Manasseh was taken there to be punished for joining in the rebellion. In Babylon, Manasseh humbles himself before the Lord and prays fervently to him. The Lord hears his prayer and restores him to Jerusalem. There he builds the outer wall of Jerusalem, strengthens the Judean army, takes away the foreign gods and altars that he had built, restores the altar of the Lord to be used for offering sacrifices, and commands the people to serve the Lord (*II Chronicles* 33:10-20). However, this brief attempt to rectify all the evil that he had seems to have been generally ineffective. Once one lives a full life of sin, a last minute repentance is hardly convincing to his fellows.

The Wicked Son of a Wicked Father—Amon (642-640 B. C.) (II Kings 21:19-26: II Chronicles 33:21-25)

Amon follows the wicked practices of his father Manasseh. He worships the idols his father had worshipped and forsakes the Lord. His servants kill him, apparently intending to seize the throne, but the people of the land avenge Amon by killing them, and make his son Josiah king.

A Start toward Restoration—Josiah (640-609 B. C.) (II Kings 22:1-23:30; II Chronicles 34-35)

In the twelfth year of his reign (ca. 628 B. C.), Josiah begins removing elements of foreign worship from Judah which Manasseh and Amon had introduced. He takes away the high places, the Asherim, and the images, breaks down the altars of the Baals, and burns the bones of foreign priests on their altars (*II Chronicles* 34:1-7).

In the eighteenth year of his reign (ca. 622 B. C.), the king has money collected to pay workmen for repairing the temple. Hilkiah the priest finds a copy of the book of the law in the temple, and sends it to Josiah. One of Josiah's servants,

Shaphan, reads it to him, and he is greatly disturbed because the book announces the overthrow of God's people because of the sins of their fathers. He sends to the prophetess Huldah to learn whether the book is authentic. She sends word back that it is authentic, and that the doom announced in it will surely come on the people of Judah; but she states that this will not occur during Josiah's lifetime because he was penitent and humbled himself before the Lord when he heard what this book said (*II Kings* 22:3-20; *II Chronicles* 34:8-23).

Josiah gathers the people to him at the temple, has the book of the law read to them, and makes a covenant to keep the commandments in this book "with all his heart and all his soul," and the people join in the covenant (*II Kings* 23:1-3; *II Chronicles* 34:29-32).

In keeping with the statutes in the book of the law, Josiah carries out the following reforms. (1) He brings out of the temple all the vessels made for Baal, Asherah, and all the host of heaven, and destroys them. (2) He deposes the idolatrous priests that the kings of Judah had ordained. (3) He breaks down the houses of the male cult prostitutes. (4) He defiles and breaks down the high places in Judah. (5) He defiles Topheth, a place located in the Valley of the Sons of Hinnom south of Jerusalem where Ahaz (*II Kings* 16:3), Manasseh (*II Kings* 21:6), and others had burned their children as sacrifices to Molech the god of the Ammonites. (6) He abolishes sun worship in Judah. (7) He destroys the altar at Bethel which Jeroboam I had built and burns the bones of its priests on it, in fulfilment of the prediction of the prophet from Judah made some 300 years earlier (*I Kings* 13:2). (8) He keeps a great Passover on the fourteenth day of the first month, according to all that was prescribed in the book of the law which Hilkiah had found. (9) He does away with all witchcraft in Judah.

Despite the fact that Josiah turned to the Lord "with all his heart and with all his soul and with all his might" (*II Kings* 23:25), apparently most of the people observe these reforms as mere external acts and are not really transformed inwardly. The Lord does not turn away his anger from Judah because of the sins of Manasseh, but declares that he will carry Judah into exile just as he had done to Israel (*II Kings* 23:4-27; *II Chronicles* 35:1-19).

In 609 B. C., Pharaoh Neco of Egypt brings his army northward along the Mediterranean coastline on his way to Carchemish to join the Assyrians against the Babylonians and their allies. Josiah decides to fight against Neco at Megiddo. Neco tries to persuade him to withdraw, but Josiah insists and is killed in the battle (*II Chronicles* 35:20-25). For the next four years, Judah is under Egyptian control.

The Work of Zephaniah and Jeremiah

The career of Zephaniah (ca. 630-624 B. C.) and part of the career of Jeremiah (627-561 B. C.) run concurrent with the reign of Josiah. Both of these prophets support Josiah's reform movement. Zephaniah declares that the "day of the Lord" is at hand, in which he will cut off the worship of Baal and of the host of heaven (*Zephaniah* 1:4-6), and Jeremiah urges the people to keep the covenant of the Lord by putting away their foreign gods (*Jeremiah* 11:1-13). At the same time, Zephaniah and Jeremiah realize that most of the people are content to keep the external acts demanded by the law without returning to God with their whole hearts, and so they urge the people to be zealous for the Lord and not "thicken on their lees" (*Zephaniah* 1:12), and to circumcise their hearts to the Lord (*Jeremiah* 4:3-4; 9:25-26). Jeremiah declares that whereas North Israel had been "faithless" to God, Judah was "false" because she did not return to him with her whole heart, but in pretense (*Jeremiah* 3:6-11).

The Fall of Assyria and the Rise of Babylon

During the reigns of Esarhaddon (681-669 B. C.) and Ashurbanipal (669-633 B. C.), Assyria enjoys considerable power in the ancient Near East. However, toward the end of the reign of Ashurbanipal and after his death, Assyria's fall and Babylon's rise come quickly. Nabopolassar of Babylon (626-605 B. C.) successfully leads the people of the city of Babylon in rebellion against Assyria in 626 B. C. In 614 B. C., the Babylonians and the Medes move north and defeat the Assyrians at Asshur. Two years later (612 B. C.), in fulfilment of the predictions of Zephaniah (*Zephaniah* 2:13-15) and Nahum (*Nahum* 3), the Babylonians move even farther north to conquer the Assyrian capital at Nineveh. Moving westward, in 609 B. C., the Babylonians defeat the Assyrians at Haran. The Assyrians retreat to Carchemish and urge the Egyptians to come to their aid for a last-ditch stand against the powerful Babylonians. Pharaoh Neco brings his army north along the Palestinian coastline in 609 B. C., and kills Josiah at Megiddo when he persists in resisting him, possibly as a political move to convince the Babylonians that Judah was her ally. From 609 to 605 B. C., Judah is under Egyptian control. Then in 605 B. C., Babylon defeats Assyria at Carchemish (see *Jeremiah* 46:2-12). Shortly thereafter, Nabopolassar dies, his son Nebuchadnezzar II becomes king of Babylon (605-562 B. C.), and Judah comes under Babylonian control.

REVIEW QUESTIONS

1. Enumerate the sins which Manasseh introduced into Judah. *II Kings* 21:1-18; *II Chronicles* 33:1-9. Discuss the reasons why this king promoted such wickedness. What lessons can modern man learn from this?

2. How did God punish Manasseh for his sins? How did Manasseh respond to this punishment? What does the Lord do? *II Chronicles* 33:10-20. Did Manasseh's actions here have lasting effects? In light of this, discuss the effect of sin on a nation's life.

3. Delineate the reforms of Josiah. *II Kings* 22-23; *II Chronicles* 34:1-35:19. What was the basis for this reform? Can any restoration movement be successful if it is not based on this foundation? Discuss the implications that Josiah's reform has for a contemporary restoration movement.

4. Relate the account of Josiah's death. *II Chronicles* 35:20-25. What may have caused Josiah to act so foolishly? Discuss.

5. Briefly describe the role that the prophets Zephaniah and Jeremiah played in Josiah's reform. *Zephaniah* 1:4-6; *Jeremiah* 11:1-13; 9:25-26; 3:6-11. What can the modern church learn from their emphasis that will be useful in attempting to restore New Testament Christianity?

6. List in chronological order the battles in which Babylon defeated Assyria. Give the dates for each battle. Locate each place on a good map. What two Old Testament prophets predicted the fall of Nineveh? How does the fulfilment of such predictions support one's faith in the inspiration of biblical speakers and writers? Discuss.

Lesson X

SIN'S WAGES-THE FALL OF JUDAH
(II KINGS 23:31-25:30; II CHRONICLES 36)

"The wages of sin is death" (Romans 6:23)

After the death of Josiah at Megiddo in 609 B. C., the kings, leaders, and people of Judah fell into great sin, and in a little more than two decades were carried into Babylonian captivity. In spite of Josiah's attempts at reformation and restoration, the apostasy of Manasseh was too deep-rooted to be exterminated. Three of the four kings who ruled in this period were sons of Josiah, and the other was his grandson. The following chart shows their relationships.

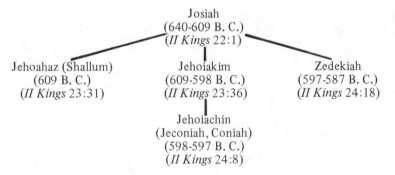

Josiah
(640-609 B. C.)
(*II Kings* 22:1)

Jehoahaz (Shallum)
(609 B. C.)
(*II Kings* 23:31)

Jehoiakim
(609-598 B. C.)
(*II Kings* 23:36)

Zedekiah
(597-587 B. C.)
(*II Kings* 24:18)

Jehoiachin
(Jeconiah, Coniah)
(598-597 B. C.)
(*II Kings* 24:8)

After Jerusalem fell to the Babylonians in 587 B. C., the Babylonians appointed them a governor named Gedaliah, who ruled as a vassal to Babylon for a brief time.

Although this period covers a relatively brief span, there are a number of important Old Testament characters that lived and worked in this era: Jeremiah, Habakkuk, Daniel,

Obadiah, and Ezekiel. Due attention must be given to them in the course of this lesson.

Jehoahaz (609 B. C.) (II Kings 23:31-35; II Chronicles 36:1-4)
When Pharaoh Neco and the Egyptians kill Josiah at Megiddo, the people of Judah make his son Jehoahaz (Jehoahaz is his throne name, Shallum is his personal name—*I Chronicles* 3:15; *Jeremiah* 22:11) king over Judah. However, Pharaoh Neco is not pleased with this, summons Jehoahaz to Riblah in the north (where he is stationed with his army waiting to aid the Assyrians against the Babylonians at Carchemish), dethrones him, and sends him to exile in Egypt, where he dies eventually. After Jehoahaz is sent into captivity, Jeremiah tells the people that he will never return to Judah (*Jeremiah* 22:10-12). Ezekiel compares him with a young lion whom the nations had taken in their pit (used as a trap) and brought to Egypt (*Ezekiel* 19:1-4).

Jehoiakim (609-598 B. C.) (II Kings 23:36-24:7; II Chronicles 36:5-8)
Pharaoh Neco makes Jehoiakim (Jehoakim is his throne name, Eliakim is his personal name—*II Kings* 23:34) the son of Josiah king in Judah. From 609 to 605 B. C., Pharaoh Neco and Egypt control Judah as a vassal. It is apparently during this period that Jehoiakim forces a number of poor laborers to build him a beautiful home, and then refuses to pay them for their work. Jeremiah rebukes him sternly for his dishonesty toward and oppression of the helpless and needy (*Jeremiah* 22:13-19). Conditions in Judah become so corrupt during this time that the prophet Habakkuk asks the Lord why he has not intervened to punish his people (*Habakkuk* 1:2-4). The Lord declares that he is about to send the Babylonians to chasten the Jews for their sins (1:5-11). This is very shocking to Habakkuk (1:12-17), but the Lord declares that he who is faithful has nothing to fear (2:1-5). Some time during the early period of Jehoiakim's reign, Jeremiah goes to the temple and condemns the worshippers who come there for trusting in the temple and all of its trappings rather than loving God with all their hearts and manifesting genuine love toward their fellowmen. He announces that Jerusalem and its temple are going to be destroyed like Shiloh and its temple, because of the great sins of the people. Jeremiah is arrested and almost sentenced to death for his message (*Jeremiah* 7, 26).

In 605 B. C., Nebuchadnezzar II and the Babylonians defeat the Assyrians and Egyptians at Carchemish (cf. *Jeremiah* 46:2-13), and Judah comes under Babylonian control. The years 605 and 604 are very important in Judean history, because in those years so many significant events occurred. Four of these may be noted here. (1) Nebuchadnezzar besieges Jerusalem and carries off many of the promising young men to Babylonian captivity to teach them the Babylonian language and culture. Among these are Daniel and his three friends, Shadrach, Meshach, and Abed-nego, who refuse to eat the king's dainties, and who excel in wisdom and understanding (*Daniel* 1). This small exile in 605 B. C. may be termed the First Stage of the Babylonian captivity. (2) Shortly after this, Jeremiah declares that because Judah has become so corrupt, God is going to keep them in captivity for 70 years, then he will bring them back to their land (*Jeremiah* 25:1-14). Thus, the 70 year exile announced by Jeremiah is to be dated from the fourth year of Jehoiakim, i. e., 605 B. C., and ends with the Jews' return to Jerusalem under Zerubbabel and Joshua in response to the decree of Cyrus king of Persia in 536 B. C. (cf. *Ezra* 1). (3) In the same year, probably because of his "temple sermon" (*Jeremiah* 7, 26) delivered sometimes between 609 and 605 B. C., Jeremiah is debarred from going to the temple, so he dictates his oracles to his amanuensis Baruch, and has him read them before the people on a fast day. The essence of his message is that Judah will be destroyed for their sins, and his purpose is to bring the people to repentance so that this disaster can be avoided. When the princes of the people hear Baruch reading this scroll at the fast the next year (604 B. C.), they bring it to Jehoiakim. As it is read to him, he cuts it into little pieces and casts it into the fire in the brazier. Jeremiah dictates another scroll to Baruch and adds new oracles to those he had included in the first scroll (*Jeremiah* 36). (4) In 604 B. C. (the second year of Nebuchadnezzar II), Daniel interprets the Babylonian king's vision of the great image. It turns out to be a panoramic view of history leading up to the establishment of the church. The head of gold is Babylon; the breast and arms of silver, Medo-Persia; the belly and thighs of brass, Greece (on the second and third figures, cf. also *Daniel* 8, especially verses 20-21, where the ram with the two horns is identified as the combined forces of Media and Persia, and the he-goat with Greece); and the legs and feet part of iron and part of clay, Rome. The stone which is cut out of the mountain without hands, and which becomes a great mountain and fills the whole earth is God's kingdom, the church, which was established during the Roman period.

That Pharaoh Neco made Jehoiakim king in place of his brother Jehoahaz may indicate that Jehoiakim was pro-Egyptian politically. In 602 or 601 B. C., Jehoiakim rebels against Nebuchadnezzar (*II Kings* 24:1), probably at the urging and promised support of Egypt (24:7). At first, Nebuchadnezzar sends bands of Chaldeans, Syrians, Moabites, and Ammonites against Jerusalem, but apparently they are unsuccessful. The Babylonian Chronicles indicate that Nebuchadnezzar himself brings the Babylonian army against Jerusalem himself in December of 598 B. C. and besieges the city. He puts Jehoiakim in fetters to take him to Babylon, but for some unknown reason Jehoiakim dies in that very month, and his son Jehoiachin is left to suffer the conse-quences of his father's rebellion. These tragic losses are due to the fact that the Lord is punishing Judah for the sins of Manasseh (*II Kings* 24:3-4).

Jehoiachin (598-597 B. C.) (II Kings 24:8-17; II Chronicles 36:9-10)
The evidence from the Babylonian Chronicles would seem to suggest that Jehoiachin's three month reign in Jerusalem was from December of 598 to March of 597. (Jehoiachin is his throne name, while Jeconiah or Coniah is his personal name). After Nebuchadnezzar besieges Jerusalem three months, Jehoiachin surrenders and is carried into Baby-lonian captivity (as Jeremiah had predicted, *Jeremiah* 22:24-22:24-30; cf. 13:18-19) with about 10,000 of the leading citizens of Jerusalem, the treasures of the temple and of the king's palace, and many of the vessels of the temple (see *Jeremiah* 27:19-22). This exile in 597 B. C. may be termed the Second Stage of the Babylonian captivity of Judah. Among those carried into exile at this time is the priest Ezekiel, who later receives his prophetic call in Babylon.

Zedekiah (597-587 B. C.) (II Kings 24:18-25:21; II Chronicles 36:11-21)
The last king of Judah is another son of Josiah and an uncle of Jehoiachin, named Zedekiah (Zedekiah is his throne

name, while his personal name is Mattaniah). Zedekiah continues the evil practices of his predecessors, and the Lord determines that now is the time to carry Judah into captivity. In ca. 594 B. C., perhaps in connection with the accession of Pharaoh Psammetichus II (594-589 B. C.) to the Egyptian throne, Edom, Moab, Ammon, and Phoenicia decide to rebel against Nebuchadnezzar, and come to Jerusalem to try to persuade Zedekiah to join them. However, Jeremiah is able to persuade Zedekiah to remain faithful to Babylon at this time (*Jeremiah* 27:1-18). Nebuchadnezzar summons Zedekiah to Babylon (*Jeremiah* 51:59), and apparently Zedekiah is able to convince him that he is still loyal to Babylon.

However, when Pharaoh Hophra comes to the throne of Egypt (589-569 B. C.) and successfully overpowers Philistia in an attack from the Mediterranean, Zedekiah rebels against Nebuchadnezzar. The Babylonian king besieges Jerusalem, and after a siege of a year and a half the city falls in July of 587 B. C. This may be termed the Third and Final Stage of the Babylonian captivity. During the siege, Hophra and the Egyptians threaten Babylon by marching from the south, but Nebuchadnezzar briefly withdraws his army from Jerusalem and repulses them (see *Jeremiah* 34:21; 37:7-11). When the Babylonians return to Jerusalem and in time break through its walls, Zedekiah tries to escape. But the Babylonians capture him and carry him north to Nebuchadnezzar, who has set up headquarters at Riblah. Nebuchadnezzar has Zedekiah's sons slain before him, puts out his eyes, and carries him into exile to Babylon, in fulfilment of the predictions of Jeremiah (*Jeremiah* 34:1-5) and Ezekiel (*Ezekiel* 12:1-13). The Babylonians break down the walls of Jerusalem, raze the temple to the ground, burn the royal palace and the houses of the city, and carry the rest of the vessels of the temple to Babylon. They leave some of the poorest people of Judah in their land as vinedressers and plowmen. When the Edomites see that the Jews are in dire circumstances, they join the Babylonians and later are able to carry off a great deal of spoil. Obadiah condemns the Edomites for helping the Babylonians in the sack of Jerusalem (*Obadiah* 11-14), and both he (*Obadiah* 1-17) and Jeremiah (*Jeremiah* 49:7-22) announce that they will be overthrown for this evil.

During the tense and critical years leading up to the fall

of Jerusalem in 587 B. C., Jeremiah continually emphasizes that the future of God's people lay with the exiles that had been carried off with Jehoiachin, and that the will of God was for those left in Jerusalem to surrender to Babylon. Among other things, he writes a letter to the exiles in Babylon who had been carried away in 597 B. C., and tells them to settle down in Babylon, and that when the seventy years (beginning with 605 B. C.) are completed they will return to Jerusalem (*Jeremiah* 29:1-14). After Jehoiachin and his fellows are carried into Babylon, Jeremiah compares them with a basket of good figs and declares that God will restore them to Jerusalem; but he compares Zedekiah and those left with him in Jerusalem, who are determined to fight against the Babylonians, with a basket of bad figs, and states that they will be overthrown (*Jeremiah* 24). During the siege of Jerusalem, Jeremiah sets before Zedekiah "the way of life" (i. e., the way to stay alive or to survive), viz., surrender to Babylon, and "the way of death" (i. e., the way to die), viz., stay in Jerusalem and fight against Nebuchadnezzar and his army (*Jeremiah* 21:1-10), but Zedekiah persists in resisting his attackers, to his own destruction.

In 593 B. C. in Babylon (*Ezekiel* 1:3), Ezekiel the priest receives his prophetic call, in which the Lord charges him to be a watchman to warn his people of the impending disaster (*Ezekiel* 3:16-21). Between 593 and 587 B. C., Ezekiel continually announces that Jerusalem will fall, hoping to bring the people to repentance, and encourages the Jews who had been carried into exile with Jehoiachin to trust in God, because the future of God's people lay with them (cf. *Ezekiel* 11:14-21). After the fall of Jerusalem, Ezekiel continues to encourage the exiles to trust in God that he would bring them back to their land (cf. *Ezekiel* 36:22-32; 37:1-14).

Gedaliah (II Kings 25:22-26)
Nebuchadnezzar leaves Jerusalem under the rule of a pro-Babylonian governor named Gedaliah. Jeremiah is given the privilege of deciding whether he will go to Babylon or stay in Judah, and he chooses the latter (*Jeremiah* 40:2-6). After some time, a group of Jews led by Ishmael murders Gedaliah. A second band of Jews led by Johanan attacks Ishmael's troops and kills many of them, but Ishmael escapes to Ammon. Possibly in fear of how Nebuchadnezzar might

react to the murder of Gedaliah, Johanan and his comrades flee to Egypt, and force Jeremiah and Baruch to go with them against their will (*Jeremiah* 40:7-43:7).

The Elevation of Jehoiachin (II Kings 25:27-30)

Archeologists have unearthed tablets in Babylon dating from the tenth to the thirty-fifth years of Nebuchadnezzar II (595-570 B. C.), which list Jehoiachin and five of his sons as recipients of rations of oil, barley, and other foodstuffs. This indicates that he was living a normal life in Babylon and was not in prison during much of this time. Even after Jehoiachin was carried into exile, many Jews believed that he would return to Jerusalem and reign in place of Zedekiah (cf. the statements of the false prophet Hananiah in *Jeremiah* 28:2-4). It is impossible to know why Jehoiachin was in prison when Evil-merodach succeeded Nebuchadnezzar on the throne of Babylon, but perhaps he tried to escape and was put in prison. At any rate, when Evil-merodach (Amel-marduk) takes the throne (561-560 B. C.), he releases Jehoiachin from prison, and Jehoiachin dines regularly at the king's table. Some 25 years later, his son Sheshbazzar (Shenazar, cf. *I Chronicles* 3:17-18) and his grandson through Shealtiel, Zerubbabel (cf. *I Chronicles* 3:17, 19; *Ezra* 3:2, 8; 5:2; *Haggai* 1:1, 12), lead the Jews back to Jerusalem for the purpose of rebuilding the temple.

REVIEW QUESTIONS

1. Name in order the last six rulers of Judah, including the governor. *II Kings* 22-25. Make a genealogical chart showing the relationships of each of these to each other (except the governor). Give the dates of the reign of each king.

2. Why was the reign of Jehoahaz so brief? *II Kings* 23:31-35; *II Chronicles* 36:1-4. What did Jeremiah and Ezekiel say about this king? *Jeremiah* 22:10-12; *Ezekiel* 19:1-4. Who was the successor of Jehoahaz on the throne of Judah? *II Kings* 23:36-24:7; *II Chronicles* 36:5-8. Who put him on the throne? How did this Judean king treat his poor laborers? *Jeremiah* 22:13-19. Discuss this carefully, and talk about modern applications of the principle laid down here.

3. Enumerate and discuss two major events in the life of Daniel and two major events in the life of Jeremiah that occurred in the years 605-604 B. C. *Daniel* 1-2; *Jeremiah* 25:1-14; 36. Elaborate on Daniel's interpretation of Nebuchadnezzar's dream of the great image, and on Jeremiah's prediction that Judah would be in captivity 70 years, making modern applications.

4. Why was Jehoiachin's reign so brief? *II Kings* 24:1, 7-17; *II Chronicles* 36:6, 9-10. Who was the Jerusalem priest that was carried into captivity with Jehoiachin? *Ezekiel* 1:1-2. When and where did he receive his prophetic call? *Ezekiel* 1:1-2; 3:16-21. What eventually happened to Jehoiachin? *II Kings* 25:27-30.

5. Briefly relate the story of Zedekiah's rebellion against Babylon, and the subsequent punishment. *II Kings* 24:20b-25:17. Who had announced that Zedekiah would be carried into Babylonian captivity? *Jeremiah* 34:1-5; *Ezekiel* 12:1-13. How does this help one believe in the inspiration of biblical writers and speakers? Discuss in light of *II Timothy* 3:16-17; *II Peter* 1:19-21.

6. What did the Edomites do when they saw the Babylonians were going to sack Jerusalem? *Obadiah* 11-14. Who were the two prophets that condemned them for this? *Obadiah* 1-17; *Jeremiah* 49:7-22. What lessons can contemporary man learn from the attitudes and punishments of the Edomites in this case?

7. What was Jeremiah's message to the exiles that had been carried away with Jehoiachin into Babylon? *Jeremiah* 29:1-14. What was his message to the Jews with Zedekiah in Jerusalem? *Jeremiah* 24; 21:1-10. Discuss.

Lesson XI

A TIME FOR REBUILDING-THE WORK OF ZERUBBABEL AND JOSHUA (EZRA 1:1-4:5; 5-6)

"Is it a time for you yourselves to dwell in your paneled house, while this house lies in ruins?" (Haggai 1:4)

Ezra 1:1-4:5; 5-6 do not deal with Ezra at all, but with events that occurred about 50 to 70 years before he returned to Jerusalem. The main concern in these chapters is the rebuilding of the temple, and the main characters who are instrumental in accomplishing this work are the prince Zerubbabel, the priest Joshua, and the prophets Haggai and Zechariah. The events recorded here took place between ca. 536 and 516 B. C.

The Rise of Persia

About 550 B. C., Cyrus II the king of Anshan (a province in Elam) overruns Astyages the king of Media, and becomes the mighty king of the massive Medo-Persian empire (550-529 B. C.). In 539 B. C., he takes the city of Babylon without a battle against Nabonidus the king of Babylon (according to the Nabonidus Chronicle). In an attempt to show that he is not a harsh and demanding ruler like the Assyrians and Babylonians before him, Cyrus restores the god Marduk to his traditional role as the god of Babylon, and decrees that all the peoples in his empire return to the lands from which they had been carried into exile, and reestablish the worship of their respective gods. In keeping with this new practice, in 538 B. C. Cyrus issues a decree that the Jews return to Jerusalem to rebuild the temple. Like other Persian documents, an official copy is written in Aramaic and placed in the royal archives at Ecbatana (Achmetha) (*Ezra* 6:2-5), and an unofficial copy is written in the language of the people involved (in this case, then, in Hebrew) and given to their leaders (*II Chronicles* 36:22-23; *Ezra* 1:1-4).

Cyrus is succeeded by Cambyses II (529-522 B. C.), who enjoys success against the Greeks and the islands of Samos and Cyprus, but who is killed by a certain Gaumata, who claims falsely that he is rightful heir to the famed Achaemenian dynasty founded by Cyrus.

Darius I Hystaspes (522-486 B. C.) rises up against Gaumata and becomes king of Persia. A record of his rise to power is preserved in his famous Behistun Inscription, which is written in Old Persian, Elamite, and Akkadian on the side of a cliff on the left side of the main caravan route from Baghdad to Teheran ca. 65 miles from Hamadan. The work of rebuilding the temple by Zerubbabel and Joshua was completed in the sixth year of his reign (516 B. C.).

The Jews return to Jerusalem and begin rebuilding the Temple (Ezra 1-3)
Seventy years after the First Stage of the Babylonian Captivity in 605 B. C. (cf. *Jeremiah* 25:1, 11-12), in keeping with the decree of Cyrus issued in 538 B. C. (*II Chronicles* 36:22-23; *Ezra* 1:1-4), in 536 B. C. the Jews under Sheshbazzar (1:8, 11; 5:14, 16) (Shenazar), son of Jehoiachin (cf. *I Chronicles* 3:17-18), return to Jerusalem to rebuild the temple. Cyrus pays part of the cost out of the royal treasury (*Ezra* 3:7; 6:4), and the Jews are to raise part of the money for this work (1:4-6). Cyrus gives Sheshbazzar and his companions many of the vessels of the temple that Nebuchadnezzar had carried into Babylon and put in the temple of his gods (1:7-11). The people who can prove their descent from their registration in the genealogies are numbered, as well as those who cannot prove their descent. Those who cannot prove it are not allowed to serve as priests. The whole assembly numbers 42,360, not including menservants and maidservants. These return to Jerusalem under the leadership of Zerubbabel the prince, the grandson of Jehoiachin, and of Joshua the priest (*Ezra* 2). In due time, Zerubbabel and Joshua build the altar of burnt offering, and offer sacrifices on it. They keep the Feast of Tabernacles (or Booths)

according to the law. They lay the foundation of the temple, and the priests and Levites with the people rejoice and praise God for what has been accomplished (*Ezra* 3).

The Jews encounter Opposition, and the Work Ceases (Ezra 4:1-5)

When the adversaries of the Jews (apparently the Samaritans and their allies, cf. verses 10, 17) see that the foundation of the temple has been laid successfully, they come to Zerubbabel and the Jewish leaders and ask to build the temple with them, but the Jews refuse. Then the adversaries discourage the Jews and hire counselors to frustrate their purpose. The work on the temple ceases from 536 to 520 B. C.

The Jews Hesitate to resume work on the Temple

The book of Haggai indicates that during the sixteen years that the Jews neglect work on the temple, they develop certain very bad attitudes which make it very difficult for them to resume the work when conditions are good for them to do so. (1) They are occupied with their own interests, including building their own homes, making a living, and increasing their wealth (*Haggai* 1:4, 6). Similarly, Jesus warns his followers not to be anxious about food, clothing, and shelter, but to seek first God's kingdom (*Matthew* 6:25-34). (2) They are stingy with their money. They realize that they must give liberally to pay the workers engaged in the building. The Lord reminds them, "The silver is mine, and the gold is mine" (2:8). (3) They are in the habit of procrastinating. Perhaps the first few months after the work ceased, the Jews felt conscience-stricken because they were not continuing this divinely appointed work. But the more they put it off, the easier it is to procrastinate. Paul admonishes Christians, "Be steadfast, immovable, always abounding in the work of the Lord, knowing that in the Lord your labor is not in vain" (*I Corinthians* 15:58). (4) The Jews are also afraid of their enemies. Perhaps they are outnumbered, or it seems that their adversaries have more influence with the Persian authorities than they. Thus, the Lord declares, "My Spirit abides among you; fear not" (*Haggai* 2:5). (5) Finally, the Jews feel that the work of rebuilding the temple is not as important as it seemed at first. Some among them had seen the temple that Solomon had built before the Babylonians had destroyed it, and they were convinced that they could never build a structure that could have as much grandeur as that. So, they reasoned, if they could not do as good a job as had been done by former generations of builders, they would not do it at all. However, both Haggai and Zechariah point out that what may seem little in the eyes of man may be very important in the eyes of God. Haggai asks: "Who is left among you that saw this house in its former glory? How do you see it now? Is it not in your sight as nothing?" (2:3), and the Lord replies, "The latter splendor of this house shall be greater than the former, says the Lord of hosts; and in this place I will give prosperity, says the Lord of hosts" (2:9). Similarly, Zechariah says: "The hands of Zerubbabel have laid the foundation of this house; his hands shall also complete it . . . For whoever has despised the day of small things shall rejoice, and shall see the plummet in the hand of Zerubbabel" (*Zechariah* 4:9-10).

The devil continually tries to discourage God's people from doing what God wants done, from building what God wants built. The reasons that the Jews gave for neglecting the work of completing the temple are repeated too often in the hearts and on the lips of Christians.

The Work of Haggai and Zechariah (Ezra 5:1-2)
The message of Haggai and Zechariah to the hesitant and indifferent Jewish workers is very simple, but very powerful: "Go up to the hills and bring wood and build the house, that I may take pleasure in it and that I may appear in my glory, says the Lord" (*Haggai* 1:8). And the reaction of the people is phenomenal. They fear before the Lord (1:12), their spirits are stirred up (1:14), they obey the voice of the Lord (1:12), and they work on the temple (1:14).

But like the prophets before them, Haggai and Zechariah are concerned with much more than merely rebuilding a physical structure. They admonish the people to center their hearts and minds on the Lord, and to treat their fellowmen with integrity and love. These words from Zechariah beautifully sum up this phase of their message: "These are the things that you shall do: Speak the truth to one another, render in your gates judgments that are true and make for peace, do not devise evil in your hearts against one another, and love no false oath, for all these things I hate, says the Lord" (*Zechariah* 8:16-17).

The Temple is Completed (Ezra 5:3-6:22)

When Tattenai, the governor of the Persian province called "Beyond the River," learns that the Jews have resumed the building of the temple, he sends a letter to Darius I. He relates that the Jews had resumed the work which had stopped sixteen years earlier, and that when he queried them about this, they told him that Cyrus II had authorized Sheshbazzar to lead the Jews back to Jerusalem and to rebuild the temple, and that he had returned to them the vessels of the temple which Nebuchadnezzar had carried to Babylon. Tattenai asks that Darius have the royal archives in Ecbatana searched to see if such a decree was ever issued (*Ezra* 5:3-17).

Darius makes the search, finds the decree, and sends a letter to Tattenai instructing him to let the Jews complete the temple, and to pay them in full and without delay from the royal revenue. The Jews continue the work and finish the temple in the sixth year of Darius (516 B. C.). They dedicate the temple amid rejoicing and the offering of sacrifices. On the fourteenth day of the first month, they keep the Passover, followed by the Feast of Unleavened Bread, according to what is written in the book of Moses (*Ezra* 6).

REVIEW QUESTIONS

1. Relate briefly some of the major events pertaining to the Old Testament during the reigns of the first three kings of Persia. *II Chronicles* 36:22-23; *Ezra* 1:1-4; 6:2-5. Name these three kings in order, and give the dates of their reigns. Do your own research on each of these kings in Bible encyclopedias and dictionaries, or in books in Old Testament history, and share what you learn with the class.

2. How many years transpired between the First Stage of the Babylonian Captivity and the return of the first group of Jews from Babylon to Jerusalem? *II Chronicles* 36:22-23; *Ezra* 1:1-4. Who predicted that it would be this long? *Jeremiah* 25:1, 11-12. How does the fulfilment of this prediction help one believe in the inspiration of God's chosen speakers and writers in Bible times? Discuss.

3. Who was the leader of the first group of Jews that returned from Babylonian exile? *Ezra* 1:8, 11; 5:14, 16. How was this man related to Jehoiachin? *I Chronicles* 3:17-18. Who were the two Jews who led in rebuilding the temple? *Ezra* 3:2, 8. How was the prince here related to Jehoiachin? *I Chronicles* 3:16-18; *Ezra* 3:2, 8; *Haggai* 1:1, 12, 14.

4. What caused the Jews to stop working on the temple after they had completed the altar and the foundation of the temple? *Ezra* 4:1-5.

5. What were the five excuses that the Jews used to neglect the continuation of the work on the temple even when conditions were favorable to do so? *Haggai* 1:4, 6; 2:8, 5, 3, 9; *Zechariah* 4:9-10. Discuss each of these excuses at length, and show how each is relevant to doing the Lord's work in any age.

6. What was Haggai's message to the procrastinating Jews? *Haggai* 1:8. Enumerate the four reactions which this message engendered in their hearts and lives. 1:12, 14. Discuss the importance of each of these in the hearts and lives of all of God's people. What was the other major emphasis in the preaching of Haggai and Zechariah? *Zechariah* 8:16-17. Discuss the importance of this in modern Christian living.

7. Who was Tattenai? *Ezra* 5:3. Give the essence of his letter to Darius I. 5:3-17. What was Darius's response? 6:1-12. When was the temple completed? 6:15. How did the Jews celebrate its completion? 6:16-22. Elaborate on the feeling that one experiences when he completes a good work.

Lesson XII

FACING CRISES IN A HOSTILE ENVIRONMENT – THE STORY OF ESTHER (ESTHER 1-10)

"Look carefully then how you walk, not as unwise men but as wise, making the most of the time, because the days are evil" (Ephesians 5:15-16)

Darius I Hystaspes was succeeded on the throne of Persia by his son Xerxes I (486-465 B. C.), the Biblical Ahasuerus. Xerxes waged large scale wars against the Greeks, and in 480 was able to cross the Hellespont and to trap the Greek fleet of ships in the Bay of Salamis. However, the naval battle that followed was disastrous to Persia, and soon Xerxes withdrew. During the rest of his reign, he was plagued by internal strifes in the Persian government. The book of Esther records events that occurred from the third (*Esther* 1:3) to the thirteenth years (3:13; 8:12; 9:1) of the reign of Xerxes (i. e., 483-473 B. C.). Thus, chronologically the life and work of Esther and Mordecai come after that of Zerubbabel and Joshua, and before that of Ezra and Nehemiah.

The events recorded in the book of Esther fall conveniently into nine scenes. The present lesson attempts to follow the unfolding story revealed in these nine scenes.

Scene I–Xerxes throws a rich party at Susa (Esther 1)
In the third year of his reign, Xerxes gives a wealthy banquet for all his princes and servants of Media and Persia at the capital, Susa (or Shushan; the modern Shush, located in southwest Iran), a very ancient city whose history covers over five thousand years, and where Darius I built a beautiful palace, which he describes on the Behistun Inscription. Xerxes' main purpose seems to have been to put everything

he had under his control on display for all to see and admire. He exhibits his riches (verse 4), his majesty (verse 4), his fineries and luxuries (verse 6), his drinks (verse 7), and his tolerant spirit (everyone was free to drink or not to drink, as he wished, verse 8). He also decides to exhibit the beauty of his wife and queen, Vashti (verses 10-11), but she refuses to come, and he becomes very angry (verse 12). He gathers together his wise men and counsellors, and they agree that Vashti must be stripped of her royal position, and that a decree must be sent throughout the land that no wife is to dishonor her husband as Vashti had attempted to dishonor Xerxes, but that all women are to honor their husbands (verses 13-22).

The biblical text does not make it clear whether Xerxes intended for Vashti to perform some lewd dance before his princes or simply come for them to admire her natural beauty. But whatever the case, one thing is clear: Xerxes viewed Vashti as a possession, as a thing, and not as a person who had the right to be private and modest about her person-hood. The tendency to use or manipulate persons to one's own ends and graitifications is devilish and anti-Christian.

Scene II—Xerxes chooses Esther as his new Queen (Esther 2:1-18)

At the counsel of Xerxes' servants, beautiful young maidens are sought throughout the Persian empire to be brought to the king's harem in Susa. The girl who pleases the king most is to be selected queen. Among the many maidens in the kingdom is a certain Hadassah or Esther, who had been raised by her much older cousin, Mordecai. Mordecai had been carried into Babylonian captivity with Jehoiachin (597 B. C.), and thus must have been about 120 to 140 during the reign of Xerxes. Esther must have been born to Jewish parents while living in exile, as she appears to be quite young when the events recorded in the book of Esther occurred.

Esther impresses Hegai, who has charge of the women in the palace, and he elevates her to the best place in the harem. However, she tells no one that she is a Jew. Mordecai checks on Esther each day to make sure she is all right. She finds favor in the sight of all who see her. Esther comes before

Xerxes in the seventh year of his reign (479 B. C.), he loves her more than all 'the women, and so he makes her the new queen.

Scene III—Mordecai saves Xerxes' Life (Esther 2:19-23)

Mordecai learns that two of Xerxes' eunuchs are planning to kill him. He sends word to Esther, Esther tells Xerxes, investigation is made, the allegation is found to be true, and the two men are hanged on the gallows. The incident is recorded in the Book of Chronicles of Persia.

Scene IV—The Elevation of Haman and his Decree against the Jews (Esther 3)

Xerxes promotes Haman above his other princes, and decrees that all bow before him when he passes by. Mordecai refuses to do this, because he believes that one should fall down and worship God alone. When Haman learns of this and that Mordecai is a Jew, he seeks a way to destroy all the Jews throughout the Persian Empire. While the lot (Pur) is being cast before him in the twelfth year of Xerxes (474 B. C.), Haman tells the king that there is a certain people in Persia whose laws are different and who do not keep the king's laws, and he asks the king to let it be decreed that they be destroyed. The following year, letters are sent by couriers that all Jews are to be destroyed on the thirteenth day of the twelfth month of that year (473 B. C.).

When selfish, worldly-minded men like Haman are rejected and do not get their way, they often become very angry and look for opportunities to avenge themselves on those who refuse to cooperate with them. However, this is not the way of Christ, who "came not to be served but to serve" (Matthew 20:28).

Scene V—Esther risks her Life to save her People (Esther 4:1-5:8)

When Mordecai learns of Haman's decree to kill all the Jews, he goes about in sackcloth mourning. Esther cannot understand Mordecai's behavior, so she sends a certain Hathach to find out what is wrong. Mordecai tells him what had happened, and gives him a copy of the decree to show Esther. He sends word that Esther must go before the king and make supplication for the Jews. Esther does not want to do this, because one cannot come before the king without being invited, on penalty of death, unless he holds out his sceptre to him. Mordecai sends word back that Esther, being a Jew, cannot escape the slaughter of the Jews which had been decreed. He expresses his conviction that if Esther keeps silence at a time like this, deliverance will come to the Jews from elsewhere. Then he adds, "And who knows whether you have not come to the kingdom for such a time as this?" (4:15).

When one views Esther's whole life, he realizes that it was hardly accidental that she was in the position in which she found herself at this critical moment. She might have been born at any period in human history, but she was born near the beginning of the fifth century; her parents might have been of any race, but they were Jews; she might have been raised by any number of people, but she was raised by Mordecai; she might never have had an opportunity to become queen in a foreign land, but Xerxes angrily cast out Vashti and Esther was the maiden whom he loved most; the Jews might never have been in danger during her lifetime, but Haman wrathfully persuaded the king to issue a decree against them. God moves in a mysterious way in the lives of individuals and nations to bring them to just that point in history when he can use them best in his purposes. Each individual needs to be alert to his divinely-given opportunities when they come, or else he will fail to realize his very purpose for being on earth.

Esther realizes that God expects her to act in behalf of her people, so she sends word to Mordecai for the Jews in Susa to hold a fast on her behalf; she resigns herself to her fate, "If I perish, I perish" (4:16). There comes a time in life when a cause or a principle or a belief is much more important than one's own life. He who realizes this and acts upon it is wise in God's eyes. Bravely, Esther goes to the king's palace, he extends his sceptre to allow her an audience, and she requests that he and Haman come to a dinner that she has prepared. When they come, she makes a second request that they come to another dinner the next day.

Scene VI—Haman's Selfishness (Esther 5:9-6:14)
Haman leaves the palace full of joy because Queen Esther

had invited him to the banquet, but when he passes Mordecai and Mordecai refuses to bow before him, he is very angry. When he arrives home, Haman gathers together his wife and friends, reminds them of all the great things he had done and received, and informs them that Esther had invited only him and the king to her banquet. When he expresses ill-feelings toward Mordecai, his wife and friends suggest that he build a gallows and the next morning tell the king to hang Mordecai on the gallows.

That night, however, Xerxes cannot sleep, so he asks that the chronicles of the kings of Persia be read to him. When the reader comes to the place that tells about Mordecai saving his life (cf. 2:21-23), Xerxes asks if anything had been done to honor Mordecai for this, and they tell him, "Nothing." Just as Haman enters the court to suggest to the king that Mordecai be hanged, the kings asks him what should be done to honor a man in whom the king delights. Thinking that the king is referring to him, Haman says he is to be clothed with royal robes, to ride on the king's horse, to wear a royal crown, and to be served by one of the king's most noble princes. Xerxes immediately commands that Haman do all this for Mordecai. After Haman has done this, he returns to his home mourning, and his wife and friends think he is doomed to fail. While they are talking, the king's eunuchs arrive to take him to Esther's banquet.

Scene VII—Esther exposes Haman's Treachery (Esther 7)
On the second day of the second banquet, Esther asks Xerxes to let her and her people be delivered, as plans had been made to exterminate them. Xerxes is shocked and asks who is responsible for this. Esther declares that it is Haman. The king storms out into the palace garden, and when he returns he finds Haman falling on the couch where Esther is, pleading with her to deliver him from the consequences of his evil deeds. However, Xerxes thinks Haman is assaulting Esther, and he has Haman hanged on the gallows that he had prepared for Mordecai.

Scene VIII—Mordecai and Esther devise a counterplan to Save the Jews (Esther 8)
Esther again takes her life in her hands by approaching Xerxes in his palace without being called, but again he

receives her by extending his sceptre to her. She asks that a decree be written allowing the Jews to defend themselves against any who might attack them on the thirteenth day of the twelfth month. Mordecai is elevated to the position formerly held by Haman, and Xerxes instructs him to send out this decree by couriers sealed with the royal seal. The Jews rejoice at this new turn of events.

Scene IX—The Jews overthrow their Attackers, and the Feast of Purim is Inaugurated (Esther 9-10)

On the thirteenth and fourteenth days of the twelfth month in the thirteenth year of Xerxes (473 B. C.), the Jews in Susa and throughout the provinces of Persia kill those that attack them. Mordecai sends letters to the Jews in all the provinces to keep the fourteenth and fifteenth days of the twelfth month as the Feast of Purim to celebrate the rest that they enjoyed after having killed those who attacked them. The reason it is called the Feast of Purim is that it was by casting lots (or Purim) that Haman had determined the day when the Jews would be exterminated; but on this very day the Jews overthrew those who intended to kill them. Mordecai has a very high position in the Persian government, and many scholars identify him with Marduka, who is known from Persian sources as a finance officer in the court of Susa during the reign of Xerxes I.

REVIEW QUESTIONS

1. Read the book of Esther through several times, and get the story firmly fixed in mind. Relate the story to other members of the class without looking at a Bible or notes. Correct one another on details.

2. Who was the king of Persia when Esther was queen? *Esther* 1:1; 2:1. What were the dates of his reign? Who was Esther's cousin who raised her from childhood and cared for her? 2:5-7.

3. Who was Xerxes' queen before Esther? *Esther* 1:9. Why was she deposed? 1:10-12. Discuss the principles involved in this deposition. Do you think Xerxes or Vashti was right? Discuss.

4. How did Mordecai save Xerxes' life? *Esther* 2:21-23. Where was a record of this kept? Under what circumstances did Xerxes become fully aware of what Mordecai had done for him? 6:1-2. How did Xerxes honor Mordecai for this? 6:6-11. Who suggested that he honor him in this way? 6:7-9. Discuss the irony of this situation.

5. Who was the Jews' enemy that had a decree issued that they be killed? *Esther* 3:8-15. What motivated him to want them exterminated? 3:2-5. How did Haman determine the day on which to exterminate the Jews? 3:7. How were the Jews delivered from this decree? 8:3-14. What feast did Mordecai and Esther ordain to commemorate this deliverance? 9:20-32.

6. Memorize *Esther* 4:13-14. Discuss the great principles revealed here that should guide Christians in their everyday walk of life.

7. Tell how Haman's selfishness was manifested when he went home to tell his wife and friends after Esther had invited him and the king alone to her second banquet. *Esther* 5:9-14. Tell how his selfishness was revealed when Xerxes asked him what should be done for one whom the king wished to honor. 6:6-9. How did these two manifestations of selfishness backfire on Haman? 6:10-11; 7:9-10.

8. Enumerate the ways in which the different events in the story of Esther reveal the providence of God at work in the lives of men and nations.

Lesson XIII

A GREAT REVIVAL-THE WORK OF EZRA AND NEHEMIAH (EZRA 4:6-24; 7-10; NEHEMIAH 1-13)

*"Wilt thou not revive us again,
that thy people may rejoice in thee?" (Psalm 85:6)*

Xerxes I is succeeded on the throne of Persia by Artaxerxes I (465-425 B. C.). During his reign, Ezra, Nehemiah, and perhaps the prophet Malachi do an important work of attempting to revive the fervor and commitment of the apathetic Jews, and to restore Judaism to the role that it had in the days of Moses and David and Solomon.

Ezra brings gifts to the Jerusalem Temple to beautify it and to Worship God (Ezra 7-8)
In the seventh year of Artaxerxes I (458 B. C.), the king commissions Ezra to go up to Jerusalem with large amounts of silver and gold to pay into the temple treasury that the temple might be beautified. He also has him take many animals to sacrifice to the Lord on the altar of burnt offering in front of the temple.

Ezra is an ideal leader for this sort of venture because of his great spiritual qualities. He had set his *heart* (a) to study God's law, (b) to do it, i. e., to obey it in his own life, and (c) to teach it to others (*Ezra* 7:10). With many years of this sort of preparation, Ezra was widely recognized as "a scribe skilled in the law of Moses which the Lord the God of Israel had given" (7:6, 12). When he gathers the Jews about him to begin the return to Jerusalem from Persia, Ezra proclaims a fast that the people might humble themselves before the

Lord, and pray for his guidance on the journey to protect them from enemies. Ezra is successful because "the hand of the Lord is upon him" (7:6, 9, 28; 8:22, 31), i. e., the Lord is guiding and protecting him in his work. Accordingly, he brings the riches and the animals to the temple that it might be beautified and that sacrifices might be offered to the Lord.

Ezra deals with the Problem of Jews marrying Foreigners (Ezra 9-10)

After the temple has been beautified and the sacrifices offered, the officials in Jerusalem come to Ezra complaining that the Jews had not separated themselves from the peoples of the lands who had led them away from God into the worship of idols. Rather, they had married foreigners. Ezra is greatly troubled (*Ezra* 9:1-3). He prays a fervent prayer to God, confessing that the Jews had sinned greatly against him, and expressing his sorrow that his fellows had broken the Lord's command (cf. *Deuteronomy* 7:1-4) not to marry foreign women (*Ezra* 9:4-15), in spite of the fact that he had given them "a little reviving" (9:8, 9).

The Jews are moved by Ezra's fervent prayer, and Shecaniah proposes that they put away their foreign wives. Ezra assembles the people to Jerusalem to carry out this decision. However, a heavy rain comes on Jerusalem at this time, and the decision is made to dismiss the people and to let this matter be handled through local leaders in the various cities and villages of Judah where they are living. A number of priests, Levites, singers, gatekeepers, and common people put away their foreign wives, but the number given in the text of the Bible is so small that it seems certain that this reform measure was not very widespread.

Nehemiah begins Rebuilding the Wall of Jerusalem (Ezra 4:6-24; Nehemiah 1-3)

The meaning of *Ezra* 4:6-24 is very difficult. It may be that after Ezra returned to Jerusalem (458 B. C.) and before Nehemiah arrived (445 B. C.), the Jews decided to try to rebuild the walls of the city and to do additional work on the temple. But the leaders of the Samaritans send letters to Artaxerxes, declaring that Jerusalem traditionally had been a hostile city that rebelled against foreign overlords, and urging him to command that the work cease. Artaxerxes issues the decree, and the work ceases.

In the twentieth year of Artaxerxes (445 B. C.), the Jew Nehemiah, the king's cupbearer, learns that Jerusalem is in shambles and the wall is not built. He asks the king to let him go to Jerusalem and rebuild the wall. Artaxerxes grants Nehemiah's request, Nehemiah goes to Jerusalem and inspects the walls, and persuades the Jewish leaders there to organize workers to accomplish this task. The Jews are very happy and begin the work. They are successful, because "the hand of the Lord is upon Nehemiah" (*Nehemiah* 2:8, 18).

Hindrances to Rebuilding the Wall (Nehemiah 4-6)

As Nehemiah works to rebuild the wall of Jerusalem, he encounters external opposition from the Samaritans and their allies and internal obstacles in the form of negative attitudes and actions on the part of the Jews. These hindrances may be conveniently enumerated.

1. *External Opposition from the Samaritans and their Allies.* (a) Sanballat, Tobiah, and Geshem deride Nehemiah and the Jews for working on the wall, and accuse them of rebelling against the king of Persia (2:19). (b) Sanballat and Tobiah ridicule the work the Jews are doing, claiming that it is a poor job and very insignificant (4:1-3). (c) Sanballat and Tobiah gather together an army to attack Jerusalem and to force the Jews to cease their working (4:7-8). (d) Sanballat and Geshem propose that Nehemiah meet with them in one of the villages in the plain of Ono (located on the southern border of the Plain of Sharon about 30 miles northwest of Jerusalem) for discussions. After Nehemiah refuses four times, they accuse him of rebuilding the wall because he plans to lead a rebellion against the king of Persia and to become the king of the Jews in Jerusalem (6:1-9). (e) Sanballat and Tobiah hire a Jew named Shemaiah to persuade Nehemiah to hide in the temple because he had learned that certain people were coming during the night to kill him. If Nehemiah had done this, Sanballat and Tobiah were planning to give him a bad reputation for being afraid of such a plot (6:10-14).

2. *Internal Obstacles on the Part of the Jews.* (a) The burden-bearers, who have to carry off the heavy bags of rubbish left in the wake of the Babylonian devastation of Jerusalem, become very tired and discouraged, and tell

Nehemiah that they are simply unable to continue (4:10). (b) One group of Jews, the Tekoites, do not put their necks to the work of their Lord (3:5), i. e., they do not work as diligently as they should. (c) Some of the Jews are exacting interest of their brethren, causing them to bear heavy financial burdens, and thus discouraging their participation in the work (5:1-8).

The work of the Lord is never done without hindrances similar to those described in connection with the work of Nehemiah as he guided the rebuilding of the wall of Jerusalem. A great deal can be learned from examining these obstacles, and also from observing the way that Nehemiah dealt with these problems. First, when his adversaries accuse him of rebelling against the king of Persia, he declares that the Lord will make the work prosper (2:20). Second, when Sanballat and Tobiah ridicule his efforts, he prays to God to overthrow them (4:4-5). Third, when his enemies threaten to fight against Jerusalem, Nehemiah has the people bring weapons to defend themselves, so that while some were building others were guarding them (4:14-23). Fourth, when Nehemiah learns that some Jews were exacting interest from their brethren, he rebukes them and persuades them to stop bringing such a heavy burden on them (5:6-19). Fifth, when Sanballat and his allies urge Nehemiah to meet with them in one of the villages in the plain of Ono, he replies that the work he is doing is so important he cannot stop to talk to them (6:3); and when Sanballat accuses him of planning a rebellion against the king of Persia because he is rebuilding the wall, he rejoinders that this idea is nothing more than the creation of Sanballat's own mind (6:8). Sixth and finally, when Shemaiah tells him of the plot to kill him and suggests that he spend the night in the temple, Nehemiah says that it would be unbecoming of him to flee (6:11). Because of Nehemiah's determination and the enthusiastic work of the people, the walls are completed in 52 days with the help of God (6:16).

Ezra and Nehemiah set matters in order in Jerusalem (Nehemiah 7:1-13:3)
After the wall is completed, there is still very much to be accomplished in order to put things on a solid footing among the Jews in Jerusalem so that they can function properly as the people of God. Ezra and Nehemiah combine their efforts

in an attempt to accomplish at least some of these things.

(a) Nehemiah appoints his brother Hanani and Hananiah the governor of the castle to rule the people in Jerusalem and to make sure that they are properly protected. Then he enrolls the people beginning with those who descended from the individuals who returned with Zerubbabel and Joshua about 90 years earlier. Those who cannot verify their genealogy are not allowed to serve as priests (*Nehemiah* 7).

(b) The Jews assemble in Jerusalem, and Ezra reads to them from the law of Moses. The Levites give the sense to help the people understand what is read (8:7-8). Nehemiah, Ezra, and the Levites teach the people (8:9), who come together to study the law (8:13). When they learn that God commanded that they keep the Feast of Booths (or Tabernacles), they do so (*Nehemiah* 8).

(c) The people separate themselves from foreigners, and confess their sins. Ezra rehearses the history of the Jews from Abraham to his own day. Throughout, he emphasizes that God had greatly blessed his people in spite of their sins (9:16, 18, 26, 29, 33). And when they sinned, he was "ready to forgive, gracious and merciful, slow to anger and abounding in steadfast love" (9:17; see also verses 19, 27, 28, 31, 32). The Old Testament, like the New, emphasizes that God by nature is forgiving and merciful (cf. *Exodus* 34:6-7; *Psalm* 103:8; *Joel* 2:13; *Jonah* 4:2) (*Nehemiah* 9:1-37).

(d) As a result of Ezra's persuasive resume of Israel's history, the people make a firm covenant in writing that they will separate from foreigners and not intermarry with them, that they will not trade on the sabbath day, and that they will perform the sacrifices and pay the tithes commanded in the law of Moses (*Nehemiah* 9:38-10:39).

(e) Because Jerusalem is so sparsely populated, many of the people move there voluntarily and lots are cast to determine others that are to move there, in order that Jerusalem might have a tenth of the population (11:1-12:26). The people dedicate the wall by forming two great companies. One goes to the right under Ezra's leadership, and the other to the left under Nehemiah's. They praise and give thanks to

God for their successes (12:27-46). On the basis of the law, they separate from Israel all of foreign descent (13:1-3).

Nehemiah executes further Reform Measures on his second trip to Jerusalem (Nehemiah 13:4-31)
In the thirty-second year of Artaxerxes (433 B. C.), Nehemiah makes a second trip to Jerusalem, and discovers that many of the Jews have reverted to their former sins. So he undertakes measures to correct these. (1) He learns that several of the Jews had married foreigners. Eliashib the priest had married the daughter of Tobiah, and had given Tobiah a chamber in the temple as his home. Nehemiah casts all of Tobiah's furniture out of the chamber, and has the temple chambers cleansed (13:4-9). Nehemiah also discovers that many of the Jews had married foreign women, so he makes them take an oath that they will put away their foreign wives lest they and their children forsake the Lord for their gods as Solomon had done (13:23-27). A grandson of Eliashib the high priest had married the daughter of Sanballat, and Nehemiah chases him off and cleanses the priesthood from everything foreign (13:28-31). (2) Nehemiah learns that the Jews had not been paying their tithes to the Levites, so the Levites had had to give up their jobs at the temple and return to their farms to survive. Nehemiah rebukes those in charge, and tithing is resumed (13:10-14). (3) Nehemiah sees Jews working on the sabbath day and trading with foreign merchants who come to the city. Thus, he has the gates of Jerusalem shut throughout the sabbath, and drives off the foreign merchants (13:15-22).

It may be that the prophet Malachi did his work in conjunction with the reforms of Ezra and Nehemiah, because he condemns the priests for desecrating the sacrifices (*Malachi* 1:6-14), and the people for marrying foreigners (2:10-12) and for failing to pay their tithes (3:6-12); and these are some of the main concerns of Ezra and Nehemiah.

REVIEW QUESTIONS

1. For what two purposes had Artaxerxes commissioned Ezra to go to Jerusalem? *Ezra* 7:14-20. What were some of the spiritual qualities of Ezra which particularly prepared him for this work? 7:10. Discuss the importance of these qualities for everyday Christian living. Why is Ezra so successful? 7:6, 9, 28; 8:22, 31. Does real success depend on this today? Discuss.

2. How did Ezra deal with the problem of Jews marrying foreigners? *Ezra* 9-10. Discuss the wisdom of Christians marrying non-Christians in light of this.

3. Enumerate and discuss the five obstacles that the Samaritans placed in the way of Nehemiah as he endeavored to build the wall of Jerusalem. *Nehemiah* 2:19; 4:1-3, 7-8; 6:1-9, 10-14. Are Christians faced with similar opposition in modern times? Discuss.

4. Enumerate and discuss the three hindrances to rebuilding the wall which came from within the Jewish community itself. *Nehemiah* 3:5; 4:10; 5:1-8. Do similar problems exist in the church today? Discuss.

5. State how Nehemiah dealt with the various problems that he confronted as he was building the wall. *Nehemidh* 2:20; 4:4-5, 14-23; 5:6-19; 6:3, 8, 11, 16. What can the contemporary child of God learn from Nehemiah's actions? Discuss.

6. Study carefully Ezra's resume of Israel's history recorded in *Nehemiah* 9:6-37. What lessons concerning the nature of God and the actions of his people can one learn from this? Discuss.

7. Discuss Ezra's efforts at teaching the people God's law. *Nehemiah* 8:1-13. What can contemporary teachers of God's will learn from Ezra's preparation (see *Ezra* 7:10) and method?

8. What three basic sins did Nehemiah have to correct among the Jews in Jerusalem on his second trip to that city? *Nehemiah* 13:4-31. Discuss each of these, and compare them with the basic teachings in the message of Malachi.

DIVIDED KINGDOM OF JUDAH AND ISRAEL
922-587 B. C.

JUDAH	ISRAEL	PROPHETS	CONTEMPORARY KINGS	CONTEMPORARY KINGS
Rehoboam (922-915)	Jeroboam I (922-901)	Ahijah Shemaiah	Shishak of Egypt (935-915)	Shishak plunders Jerusalem (918)
Abijam (915-913)				
Asa (913-873)	Nadab (901-900)	Azariah Hanani		War with Baasha. League with Benhadad I of Syria.
	Baasha (900-877)	Jehu	Zerah the Cushite Benhadad I of Syria (880-842)	
	Elah (877-876)			
	Zimri (876)			
	Omri (876-869)		Ithobal, king of Tyre and Sidon	
Jehoshaphat (873-849)	Ahab (869-850)	Micaiah Elijah Eliezer		Battle of Ramoth-gilead Battle of Qarqar (853)

JUDAH	ISRAEL	PROPHETS	CONTEMPORARY KINGS	CONTEMPORARY KINGS
	Ahaziah (850-849)	Elisha		
Jehoram (849-842)	Jehoram (849-842)		Mesha, king of Moab	Benhadad I besieges Samaria
Ahaziah (Jehoahaz) (842)			Hazael in Syria (842-805)	
Athaliah (842-837)	Jehu (842-815)			
Joash (837-800)				
	Jehoahaz (815-801)			
	Jehoash (801-786)		Benhadad III of Syria	
Amaziah (800-783)	Jeroboam II (786-746)	Jonah (II Kings 14:25) Amos (750)		

95

DIVIDED KINGDOM OF JUDAH AND ISRAEL (3)

JUDAH	ISRAEL	PROPHETS	CONTEMPORARY KINGS	CONTEMPORARY KINGS
Uzziah (Azariah) (783-742)		Isaiah Hosea (745)	Tiglath-pileser III (Pul) 745-727	
	Zechariah (745)			
	Shallum (745)			
	Menahem (745-738)			
	Pekahiah (738-737)			
	Pekah (737-732)			
Jotham (750-735)		Isaiah (742-700)	Rezin, king of Syria (740-732)	Syro-Ephraimitic War (734-732) Fall of Damascus (732)
Ahaz (735-715)	Hoshea (732-724)		Shalmaneser V, king of Assyria (727-722) Sargon II, king of Assyria	Israel carried into the Assyrian captivity. (721) Sargon II's siege of Ashdod. (711)

96

JUDAH	ISRAEL	PROPHETS	CONTEMPORARY KINGS	CONTEMPORARY KINGS
Hezekiah (715-687)		Micah (725-700)	Sennacherib, king of Assyria (705-681)	Sennacherib besieges Jerusalem. (701)
Manasseh (687-642)		Nahum (614-612)	Esarhaddon, king of Assyria (681-669)	
Amon (642-640)				
Josiah (640-609)		Zephaniah Jeremiah (626-575)	Nabopolassar, king of Babylon, (626)	Battle of Ashur (614) Battle of Nineveh (612) Battle of Haran (609) Battle of Megiddo with Pharaoh-Necho (609)
Jehoahaz (609)		Zephaniah Jeremiah		
Jehoiakim (609-598)		Habakkuk (605)	Nebuchadnezzar, king of Babylon (605-562)	Beginning of Babylonian captivity (605). Battle at Carchemish (605)
Jehoiachin (598-597)				Second conquest of Jerusalem and deportation (597)
Zedekiah (597-587)		Ezekiel (593-573)	Pharaoh-Hophra, king of Egypt (588-569)	Destruction of Jerusalem (587)
				Jehoiachin's elevation by Evil-merodach (561)

BIBLIOGRAPHY

Literally thousands of books and articles have been written on various historical, linguistic, archeological, and theological aspects of the period from Jeroboam I and Rehoboam to Ezra, Nehemiah, and Malachi in a wide variety of modern languages. In a general sense, the reader may be pointed to certain specific Bible encyclopedias which contain numerous articles pertaining to specific issues covered in these centuries, such as *The Interpreter's Dictionary of the Bible* (four volumes, with a fifth Supplementary Volume), J. L. McKenzie's *Dictionary of the Bible,* and the *Wycliffe Bible Encyclopedia* (2 volumes); as well as to standard commentaries such as *Peake's Commentary on the Bible, The Jerome Biblical Commentary, The Interpreter's Bible, The Interpreter's One-Volume Commentary on the Bible,* and the commentaries of J. Gray on I-II Kings in the *Old Testament Library* series, Curtis on I-II Chronicles, Batten on Ezra and Nehemiah, and Paton on Esther in the *International Critical Commentary,* and J. M. Myers on I-II Chronicles, Ezra, and Nehemiah in the *Anchor Bible* series, along with standard histories of the Old Testament by Bright, Herrmann, and Noth, and Old Testament theologies such as those of W. Eichrodt (2 volumes), G. von Rad (2 volumes), and T. H. Vriezen.

In addition to these, the following studies are helpful and challenging on specific issues.

Albright, W. F. *From the Stone Age to Christianity.* Garden City, N. Y.: Doubleday & Co., Inc., 2nd edition, 1957.

Bickerman, E. J. "The Edict of Cyrus in Ezra 1," *Journal of Biblical Literature,* 65 (1946), pp. 244-275.

Childs, B. S. *Isaiah and the Assyrian Crisis.* London: SCM Press Ltd., 1967.

Cook, H. J. "Pekah," *Vetus Testamentum,* 14 (1964), pp. 121-135.

Rowley, H. H. "Hezekiah's Reform and Rebellion," *Men of God.* New York: Thomas Nelson & Sons, 1963, pp. 98-132.

Rowley, H. H. "Nehemiah's Mission and Its Background," *Men of God.* New York: Thomas Nelson & Sons, 1963, pp. 211-245.

Rowley, H. H. "The Chronological Order of Ezra and Nehemiah," *The Servant of the Lord and Other Essays.* Oxford: Blackwell, 1965, pp. 135-168.

Thiele, E. R. *The Mysterious Numbers of the Hebrew Kings.* Grand Rapids, Mich.: Wm. B. Eerdmans Publishing Co., revised edition, 1965.

Wiseman, D. J. *Chronicles of Chaldean Kings (626-556 B. C.) in the British Museum.* London: British Museum, 1956.